BASIC
SIGIL
MAGIC

BASIC
SIGIL
MAGIC

PHILLIP COOPER

WEISER BOOKS

York Beach, Maine, USA

First published in 2001 by
Weiser Books
P.O. Box 612
York Beach, ME 03910-0612
www.weiserbooks.com

Library of Congress Cataloging-in-Publication Data

Cooper, Phillip
    Basic sigil magic / Phillip Cooper.
        p. cm.
    Includes bibliographical references and index.
      ISBN 1-57863-207-2 (pbk. : alk. paper)
    1. Sigils.   2. Color—Miscellanea.   3. Magic.   I. Title.

    BF1623.S5 C66 2001
    133.4'3—dc21   00-068576

VG

Typeset in 11 pt. Palatino
Cover design by Ray Rue

Printed in the United States of America

08 07 06 05 04 03 02 01
8 7 6 5 4 3 2 1

The paper used in this publication meets all the minimum requirements of the American National Standard for Information Sciences–Permanence of Paper for Printed Library Materials Z39.48–1992 (R1997).

CONTENTS

INTRODUCTION

AS WE EMBARK ON A NEW AGE AND WONDER what the future may hold for us, it is a time to reflect on the past. We were previously in the age of Pisces. Pisces rules, among other undesirable things, prisons and restrictions. Pisces dawned—with promises of a fairy-tale existence, the great oneness of humankind, and the kingdom of heaven on Earth—with the birth of Christ. There are numerous connections to the sign of the fish at this time. The secret symbol for the early Christians was the fish, Jesus was called Ichthus (the fish), and many of his disciples were fishermen.[1]

Each age has certain characteristics and traits associated with its sign. With the end of the Piscean age, we can see that its promises were not fulfilled. The races are more divided than ever, in spite of diplomatic, political, and religious cosmic surgery. The burden of sin and guilt taught by the world's religions weighs far more heavily than it ever has. Far from relieving humankind of its burden, these religions have set it, and more, firmly and squarely on our shoulders. Heaven must have taken a wrong turn as it descended to Earth, because it never arrived.

We will only survive the metamorphosis of the new age, if we can let the past go. The transition from old to new will

---

[1] David Geddes and Ronald Grosset, *Astrology & Horoscopes* (New Lanark, Scotland: Geddes & Grosset, 1997), p. 21.

not be easy. Almost everyone is familiar with the twelve signs of the zodiac and the fact that they each cover approximately one month of our solar year. An age is approximately two thousand years. Each sign of the zodiac corresponds to a 2000-year period, making a total of 24,000 years to complete the cycle. That 24,000 year cycle is called a Great Year, or Aeon. Our twelve-month Earth zodiac starts in Aries and goes forward—Taurus, Gemini, and so forth, through Pisces. The Great Year cycle, however, starts in Aquarius and goes backward—Capricorn, Sagittarius, and so forth. This makes the arrival of the Age of Aquarius rather more significant, as it is not only the beginning of a new age, but also the beginning of a new aeon. It is not only the end of one age and the transition to the next, it is the end of one Great Year and the beginning of another. Indeed, the new age, the Age of Aquarius (2000–4000 A.D.) is upon us. The signs can already be seen in the strong presence of new sciences and technology, and space travel. The techno-age is upon us, and with it comes a new magick and new approaches to magick.

Since the early 1980s, when chaos theory emerged in the physical sciences, a similar theme has sprung up in the field of magick. This new magick is difficult to define, as it has very few boundaries and those that exist are put there by individual practitioners. The magician is not guided into using any fixed magical ideas, as this new Aquarian techno-age magick accepts that there is no single authoritative way of doing things. Magick can be practiced in many ways. The emphasis is on the practice itself.

Today, many people are familiar with the almost mystical concept of chaos theorists that "a single butterfly beating its wings in China can set off a sequence of events culminating in global weather patterns on the other side of the world and so on."[2] What this means is "it's easier to bring about a small change in the universe than a huge one." The universal

---

[2] James Gleick, *Chaos: The Amazing Science of the Unpredictable* (London: Minerva, 1997), p. 9.

uncertainty that chaos physics brings into our worldview is not new. To quantum physicists, it has been the bane of their profession at the sub-atomic level. What the discovery of the possibilities raised by chaos theory has done is to reinstate the magical paradigm of the the acausal connection of events at the macroscopic level—a paradigm which science insists has to be satisfied if magick is to be taken seriously. No longer must there be "a tremendous input of energy," provided the magician has done a thorough job of analyzing when and where to magically "nudge" the unfolding event. If this is so—and indeed it is—then your future is in your own hands. Changing the future is what magick is all about. The past is gone. It is unalterable. The present is here and is also unalterable. However, the future is not, as yet, in existence and can, therefore, be influenced.

Many of the techniques of modern New Age magick do not involve the complex ritual regalia and exacting periods of preparation used in traditional ceremonial magick. Contrary to popular belief, this new magick is not a disorganized "make-it-up-as-you-go-along" pursuit. The magician learns when certain techniques are applicable and when they are not. Spontaneity has a place in ritual. Effectively, New Age magicians use whatever works best, mixing and borrowing from existing magical systems or inventing new techniques, even though there is an old magical law that states that you should never mix traditions. This is not to say that ancient or medieval theories have been discarded. This would be like removing the foundations of a building. Without them, disintegration would be inevitable. Ancient and medieval magick acted as steppingstones from the ancient to the modern tradition.

Magick is all about perfecting magical practices so that the magician can get the best out of life. This new magick is famous for developing certain techniques. These include Austin Osman Spare's methods of sigil magick. What is sigil magick? Contained in this modern grimoire is a tried, proven, and practical paradigm for sigil magick. Rather than burden you with more far-fetched arcane theory, this book can save you a fortune in money and a lifetime of heartbreak. It provides a model of concentrated living magick that can make things happen when you become adept at it. Theory follows practice. As with any kind of magical technique, trying it out and discovering for yourself that magick works is worth any amount of theoretical discussion.

This book is written in two parts. The first part, The Psybermancer, is an exegesis on the theory and practice of sigils. Here I explain and expand the practices and principles developed by the English mage, Austin Osman Spare. The Psybermancer explains magical gnosis, the sleight-of-mind techniques of sigilization, as well as full rituals, opening and closing techniques, the four gateways of power, and mantras and dervish whirling. All of these create the most powerful rites. Whether you are new to the subject or already familiar with the magical process of sigilization, I hope you will find this book of great value.

Part II, The Psybernomicon, details and classifies different types of magick by color. It gives an eightfold division of magick that can be attributed to the seven classical planets, plus Uranus for the magical self. Naturally, magick itself has no color. These are merely associative devices.

The paradigm in this book relates to what is termed Orphic Magick—that is, an emotional approach, in contrast to Hermetic Magick, which uses the mind to work magick. In recent times these have been divided into two broad categories of "inhibitory" and "excitatory gnosis."[3] Hermetic Magick is inhibitory; Orphic Magick is excitatory. The classification is not absolute, and magical practitioners usually find, on a personal level that some techniques work better than others, or that particular techniques for inducing gnosis are more effective than others when applied to some specific in-

---

[3] Magical practitioner Peter Carroll, who is considered the foremost exponent of modern Chaos Magick, divided these into two broad categories of gnosis in his book, *Liber Null & Psychonaut* (York Beach, ME: Samuel Weiser, 1987), p. 31.

tent. However, all magical techniques that work always have a combination of emotional content and mental discipline, regardless of category.

In the chapters that follow, you will be shown how to use sound magical techniques to enhance your life. They are based on the philosophy of life that will be given to you throughout this book and are safe and natural. If followed carefully, with dedication and patient practice, they will be instrumental in transforming your life and giving you a better understanding of life in general. The only condition is that *you* must make the effort by studying and applying these techniques. Always remember that magick is not a hobby. It is a way of life and, if used properly, it will reward you by giving you power to change your life in ways that will surprise you.

Part I

The Psybermancer

INITIATION INTO MAGICK

WELCOME TO THIS VERY SPECIAL BOOK that deals with the magical process of sigilization! It is unlike any other book of instruction, insofar as it attempts to present the truth about magick and open an individual path to the inner mysteries. In order to derive maximum benefit from this book, it is essential that you proceed slowly and carefully, thinking deeply about the paradigms presented to you. Despite ideas given in certain types of literature, there is no such thing as "instant" magick—no rapid path to enlightenment. Patience is, therefore, the motto to be adopted.

If I had to give you a single key—words that would serve as your guide to real magick—it would be:

Input = Output

A major law of the cosmos states that you get "out" in direct proportion to that which you put "in." The ratio is invariable. Also, note that time and money are not necessarily the criteria. It is the quality of the input that matters.

Social Magick:
Forming a Group and Making a Covenant

The bringing together of two or more people to perform rituals has certain advantages, as long as personality clashes are avoided. Working rites with incompatible people is a complete waste of time, so get to know others first. If there is common ground, nurture it. Any group rite has to have a common objective, whether knowledge or acquisition, if it is to survive. A basic constitution should be drawn up before any ritual work is undertaken, no matter how simple or basic the work may be. Rites should be planned so that each person can function as an individual within the whole, and so that the end product will benefit all. Don't let one person run the whole show, with everyone else following. There should be a cadre of adepti whose job it is to teach others. As such, they should operate only with members on their own level, or for instructive purposes. In ritual magick, everyone should have their turn at taking every role in temple rites, seasonal ceremonies, and initiations, otherwise a magical lodge becomes a "cult" in the worst sense of the word. With four people, for example, you may have four officers, each one taking responsibility for one element and its doorway, a fact that can be used for any ritual, especially those designated as seasonal.

A seasonal rite is one that is dedicated to a season of the year, whose purpose may be attunement, learning, acquisition, or all of these. A rite at spring, for instance, may be performed around the time of the spring equinox. Its aim might be the planting of an idea that would bear fruit in the autumn. This idea can be carried around the seasons, at each of the four points of tidal change.[1] Seasonal rites are very useful, both for

---

[1] The four points of tidal change occur when the ecliptic and the celestial two sphere lines cross twice, at the vernal and autumnal equinoxes, otherwise known as the March equinox (or first point of the sign of Aries) and September equinox (or first point of the sign of Libra). The two points at which the ecliptic is farthest from the celes-

groups and for the individual worker who wishes to under-stand the way in which nature works.

Group working differs from solo work on many points, and you will have to get together to work out a plan of the rite, right down to the last detail, so that everyone knows what is going on and knows what they are to say and do. A script will have to be drawn up. This should be memorized, so that every officer says meaningful things at the right time—not an easy task, but one that is well worth the time and effort involved. In doing so, you not only get involved in the rite, you also learn a great deal. At the end of a group rite, useful comparisons of inner visions and feelings can be made, and other ideas can be discussed. All conjurations, path-working scenarios, and rituals should be known and standardized.

The Individual Path to Self-Initiation

Whether you are part of a group or work solo, in the final analysis, the only realistic magical path is one of individual effort that leads to truth. A person can no more work magick for you while you reap the rewards, than a person can eat your food for you while you enjoy it! If we return to the initial idea of input = output, here you are dealing with the highest quality of input. The resulting output is bound to be ideal and more in keeping with your true path in life.

Never treat your magical work as some sort of hobby or part-time interest you fit in whenever you can spare a little time. The input = output law is bound to give you proportional results that are bound to be disappointing. Similarly, you can learn from others and, in some instances, work with other people, provided that you do not give up individuality and freedom.

---

tial equator are called the solstices, and these occur in June for the summer solstice (when the sun enters Cancer) and December for the winter solstice (on entering Capricorn). In the southern hemisphere these equinoxes and solstices mark the reverse situation.

Your Magical Self

You are an individual. There is no one else like you in existence, so it naturally follows that there is only one path for you to follow—your own. This path leads to truth—not someone else's truth, but your own truth concerning your magical real self and your relationship with the universe. No teacher can ever lead you to this truth. All that can ever be done is to show you the way. This is done by giving you a realistic pattern of perfection based on universal truths—for example, those laws that apply to everyone, whatever their individual paths may be. You have already been given one such law. It applies to everyone and yet it allows total freedom of expression, for such is the nature of cosmic law and truth.

Truth

What is truth? A realistic definition is that truth is the discovery of your real self, your inherent potential, and your relationship with the universe. By discovering the truth about yourself, you gain freedom and acquire power. This is a goal worth aiming for.

Self-Initiation

The word "initiate" simply means "to start." The moment you start to search for truth in any way, shape, or form, you have actually started on the path of initiation. From then on, your initiation deepens in direct proportion to your efforts. Remember, input = output.

There are many stages on a path. Each one is an initiation in itself, as certain realizations are made. Again, these are personal realizations and are dictated by your own progress and level of advancement. These levels, incidentally, have nothing whatsoever to do with the grades and titles adopted by lodges and covens. An initiate advances by becoming aware.

The Choice of Path

There are, as you will no doubt discover, many misconceptions in magick, largely due to carelessness and lack of thinking. In magick, there are two main paths to follow—practical magick and esoteric magick.[2] The former, by its very name, implies getting physical results from magical workings. The latter is concerned with the subject of magick in its own right. A person may, by free choice, follow either or both paths. In fact, it is a poor magician who cannot control or understand the physical end of life or try to understand its inner mysteries.

Often you will hear of "left" and "right" paths, of the evils of "materialism" and of black or white magick. I will now set out the truth of the matter and then you must judge for yourself.

Materialism

There is a mistaken idea, especially among the devotees of "high" magick, that the material side of life is evil and is to be resisted. This is silly. You live in a physical world and, unless you take control of the physical side of life, it will control you. There is no compromise—control or be controlled, that is the law.

There are many reasons why the material world came to be despised. Most of these restrictive ideas came from Eastern philosophies in which poverty is held up as a mark of spirituality and deprivation as a sure sign of success. Christianity carried on the dubious tradition, adding its own dimension to an already invalid belief.

---

[2] Practical magick equates to so-called low magick and is primarily concerned with the use of magical techniques to obtain solid, physical results. The other side of the coin is esoteric magick which equates to high magick and is the path to follow if you would study magick as a subject in its own right.

To regard the material side of life as evil is absurd. There is nothing wrong with it in itself. What is wrong is the approach. Most people simply do not understand that they can have virtually anything they desire simply because they are entitled to have these things. It is only when the wrong attitudes, such as greed, jealousy, envy, and other negative ideas, take over that trouble begins. Once people realize that, when they ask of life, instead of stealing from others, they will receive all that they need, the problem ceases.

The truth about physicality and your ability to bring abundance into your life belongs to the realms of practical magick. It is vital that you do not consider the material side of life evil or beneath you. To think like this is to subscribe to a doctrine of hopelessness and defeatism. It should be remembered that, in the past, every time there was a mistake or catastrophe, it was blamed on the gods, who, in turn, became an excuse for failure. This turned into a vicious circle that gradually evolved into the now familiar scapegoat of the "will of the gods." The crux of the matter is that most people use this as a ready-made excuse for failure and lack. People can and do blame all sorts of intangibles for their own failure. So-called "enlightened" leaders continue to teach this absurd philosophy.

Left and Right

The ideas just mentioned have spilled over into magick in many ways. Perhaps the most obvious example is found in the idea of "right-hand" and "left-hand" paths. This has caused an artificial division in magick. Anyone who uses magical paradigms to enhance their own life is said to be on the left-hand path. The opposite, or right-hand, path is exclusively reserved for those who are supposed to be spiritual. The less enlightened simply blanket all this with the words black or white magick.

The use of magical paradigms to influence the material world is perfectly valid. In fact, we all influence physicality all the time without realizing it. Instead of using hackneyed phrases such as black and white, and assuming that one is beneath the other, it would be more sensible to look for the truth first, and then make judgments. It is regrettable that very few practitioners do think. Instead, they simply accept that which appears obvious and then try to make it work.

Good and Evil

There is no such thing as "good" and "evil." Think about this carefully, because it happens to be true. What is good for one person is not necessarily good for another. The same is true of the word "bad." In reality, it is all a question of choice. Remember that you can exercise unrestricted free choice in any area of your life. In doing this, however, you may affect others in ways that appear to be "bad."

On an individual level, you must be the judge of your intentions and try to ensure that you do not knowingly harm others in the process. As in any situation, you must look at the facts that contribute to a decision, then act on them. The facts, however, may well be wrong, and you may, without knowledge, affect someone adversely. In either case, you could be judged to be "wrong." This is unfortunate, but it does happen. By gaining more insight or wisdom, however, you can learn to make fewer mistakes. It is quite another matter to deliberately persist in a course of action that you know to be bad, detrimental, or wrong. Not only are you violating the rights of others, you are damaging yourself in the process.

In the final analysis, the best way to view good and evil is not by accepting the religious definitions of these words. It is better to be more realistic and sensible. Forget about retribution, sin and other false concepts. Instead, apply common sense and sound reasoning.

The Science of Magick

Esoteric magick is concerned with inner truths, as opposed to the more day-to-day issues covered by practical magick. As such, it is not higher or more noble. It is merely a different path. A fair analogy might be to compare practical magick with flying an aircraft and esoteric magick with designing it. Both are necessary; both are equally important. So it is with the two main branches of the art. In practical magick, you are concerned with getting results, while in esoteric magick, you desire to know how.

Universal Laws

Magick is a valid art, not a pseudo-science, and should be treated as such. Its existence cannot be proved or disproved in a high school physics lab. As in any science, you have to check your theories, sift through facts, and only adopt sane and rational ideas. You have to be scientific in the highest sense of the word.

One of the greatest problems with today's magick is that, far from being scientific, it has degenerated into a shambles of superstitions, muddled thinking, and the wholesale acceptance of unfounded ideas. Rather than go into detail at this stage, I will continue to point out these problems as we come to them.

The Cosmic Paradigm

In reality, there is no such thing as God. There is only energy. This energy is not random or chaotic; it is ordered and conforms to precise laws. The ultimate conclusion must be that there is intelligence behind energy and that this intelligence can be approached and contacted. This concept makes the classical image of God inadequate.

At the opposite end of the scale there is "you." What relationship do you have with the energies of life? The answer is that you have unlimited use of these energies and total free choice in the way in which you use them. This may, at first, seem quite illogical and untrue—that is, until you look a little deeper.

Looking beyond the obvious is what magick is all about. It is the truth, not facts, that you seek and you will rapidly learn that the apparent facts are not always true. It is thus folly to use them as a basis for belief. The only equation that successfully explains your true relationship to life energy is:

YOU = YOUR BELIEF PARADIGMS = ENERGY

This apparently simple statement will, if you think deeply about it, explain all of life's problems and, equally, give you the key to vast reserves of power. You are a creative being who uses life energy and directs it according to your will— whatever that may be. There are no restrictions or limitations other than those that are believed. The word "belief" is a major factor, as you will see. Everything that exists in your life is a direct result of your beliefs. Nothing happens by chance, nor are events controlled by fate or absurd concepts, such as karma. It is all there because you willed it to be so, either knowingly or unknowingly.

Anything that is accepted or believed affects the subconscious mind—that part of you which has the ability to direct energy and, thereby, achieve physical results. It knows no limits, nor does it recognize restrictions and limitations in the normal sense. In short, give it an instruction (belief) and it will carry this out to the letter. It naturally follows that, if your beliefs are wrong or self-limiting, you are bound to get the equivalent in physical results. Input = output. Your problems are not, therefore, due to external causes, they are entirely internal. It is impossible to overestimate the power of the subconscious mind. Not only will it carry out every command you give it, but it will also answer all questions.

Everything in existence contains energy in numerous patterns. Matter without energy is inert and useless. In order to understand the nature and workings of this energy, you must find some means of dividing it into convenient units. There are several systems that attempt to do this. By far the best is the

Cabbalistic Tree of Life. This incredible system helps us categorize energy and indeed everything else in life.

The only thing to bear in mind, for now, is that the only difference between, say, an orange and a lump of rock, are the different patterns of energy each contains. Also, if you know the type and nature of energy pattern inherent in an object, you are bound to have an understanding of the object and, more important, control over it.

The Magical Trident

Access to the knowledge and power of the subconscious mind comes through three means:

- The mind;
- The emotions;
- The imagination.

These are the points of the trident. The handle equates to the will. Briefly, to activate the subconscious, there first has to be an intention. For example, something must be willed. This is then directed into subconscious levels through either or all of these three access points. Sustained will is equivalent to belief and belief always gets results. The use of these three approaches will be discussed in detail later on.

Cause and Effect

Anything that you cause to happen must have an effect. The law of cause and effect is perfect and cannot be disputed or bypassed. You and no one else are totally responsible for the instructions you give to your subconscious mind—hence the need for caution and forethought. Never dabble in magick or play games with your subconscious, or you may activate a response that is hard to control. Good technique is vital to successful magical practice. Take responsibility for your actions and practice magick responsibly.

In addition, it is in your own interest to root out all belief patterns that are not in your best interests, because these can cause problems deep within your subconscious mind. This is one reason why the mysteries stress the maxim, "Know thyself." In other words, get to know all parts of yourself, even the bad parts, so that you can correct them. The problems you have had to face in life are entirely due to cause and effect. They are not caused by some vengeful god, intangibles such as fate and karma, or by anything or anybody else. You are the cause and, therefore, you must experience the effect. Naturally, the reverse is also true. Life is really what *you* make of it.

Conscious Control and Blocks

When directing power to acquire a definite result, there are two factors involved: the conscious control of power, and the blocks that prevent the effective use of power. Each person has any number of these blocks or habits. They manifest as fears, phobias, compulsions, strange ideas, and beliefs or nonbeliefs that you have accepted without thinking. Magick can only be effective when all the blocks are realized and replaced by truth. This truth is different for each person, as everybody has a different point of view and no two people see the same thing in the same way. In the past, these blocks were conceived of as demons, in the same way that angels represented the higher aspects. If you wish to use the visual image of a demon or an angel (better known as a "telesmatic image"), then do so, but keep in mind what they really are or serious error will result.[3] These things are not real and are not to be given any unwarranted importance. The idea of bowing the knee to an angel or fleeing from a demon is ridiculous.

---

[3] These are personifications of some desirable quality or power; an image of a being with whom you can converse, which is repeatedly built up over a period of time in the imagination. The Cabbalistic archangels are a good example of this. Much is to be gained from this technique provided that you do not credit this imaginary being with power over you.

Although some magical traditions portray our compulsive savage instincts as demons and the cosmic entities as angels, these are merely labels that describe the dual aspects of a single universal intelligence. The Church used rituals such as baptism, and hard monastic discipline in order to subdue our instincts. Whatever you choose to call the demonic aspects of the self, they are real enough to defeat logic and determine both individual and social conduct. In the invocation of the so-called Holy Guardian Angel, the lower self (in other words, the undesirable blocks) is made to prostrate itself to the higher true self. As long as you bear in mind that this is all a metaphor for the Self, all is well and good. The paradigm falls down when the Holy Guardian Angel is seen as something outside the Self, and the operator identifies with the lower self. Feelings of guilt and worthlessness come from the lower self and are encouraged in many religions and esoteric schools—a victory for the lower self.

You are evolved; you have power. All you have to do is rediscover it. Tackle each block as you come to it. If something appears not to work, then there is a reason for this. Blocks to completion lie within the magician or the recipient (you can't blame failure on God). For example, a ritual for healing will not work if the recipient does not truly desire healing. Humans have wills of their own. It may take a long time for you to discover your blocks, but it is all a question of effort; the more you look for them, the quicker you will be rid of them. Magick, like every practical initiatory system, starts when you subdue the primitive instincts that govern your behavior. Only then is a positive relationship with the cosmos possible.

The assertive "demonic" element of the human brain, or the lower self, knows and uses our weaknesses to anticipate every challenge to its dominance. So determination alone is not enough. A sequential strategy is necessary to overcome your blocks and we will fully deal with this in the next chapter.

2

CRITICAL
SELF-ANALYSIS

THERE ARE MANY PROBLEMS THAT ACT as "blocks" to power; some are obvious, others are not. To begin with, the most powerful part of yourself is your mind, which can also be your worst enemy, if left to its own devices. Any serious magician worthy of the name must realize that in order to increase the chances of success and improve the quality of his or her work, he or she must gain mastery over the mind. By this I do not simply mean the subconscious mind, I mean the *conscious* mind, for this is where most of the difficulties start. Valuable though it is, the conscious mind is often the very thing that gets in the way both before, and during, a magical operation.

The Great Law of Tenfold Return

Followers of magick should be dedicated to attaining a high degree of self-discipline and control over all levels of their personal sphere of existence—physical, mental, emotional, spiritual, and subconscious—and they must also control the channels by which they are linked to the rest of humanity. Negativity, superstition, fear, and imbalance must be erased from the outer personality and from inner reality. What is erased from within cannot attract from without. Those who are afraid will attract fear. Those who are hateful will attract hate.

Everybody has a reptilian brain kernel (diencephalon), which predates humankind by countless millions of years, and which still responds to the cycles of nature.[1] It has three compulsive survival urges: feeding, fighting, and sex. However advanced human society imagines itself to be, and no matter how it rationalizes its behavior, these three primordial instincts still dictate the destiny of individuals and nations. They are the demons that Solomon is said to have imprisoned with magical seals.[2]

Every working magical system seeks to constrain demonic forces in service of the true will. This important aspect of magick is the process of separating the spiritual gold (the angelic persona) from the human dross (the demonic persona). Anger, hatred, envy, greed, lust, fear, are emotions that control humankind; man and woman are completely at their mercy. How many times have you been angry and said something hurtful to a loved one? You may have said or done it in the heat of the moment and been thoroughly ashamed of yourself afterward. Yet, at that moment in time, you could not control your emotions; they controlled you like a puppet. People have killed in that uncontrolled moment, and all the shame and remorse in the world will not right the wrong.

At first, the magician must think about, analyze, and consciously control every thought, word, deed, and emotion. This is hard work, but in time, it becomes second nature. When the magician reaches a balanced state, then the real work begins.

[1] Frater U. D., *Practical Sigil Magic: Creating Personal Symbols for Success* (St. Paul, MN: Llewellyn, 1990), p. 85.

[2] See Aleister Crowley, ed., and S. L. MacGregor Mathers, trans., *The Goetia: The Lesser Key of Solomon the King* (York Beach, ME: Samuel Weiser, 1995).

Inner balance and harmony are not only achieved, but multiplied. This is the great law of tenfold return.

Critical Self-Analysis

In order to gain power, you must first start by looking at the way you think in everyday life. Look at the way in which you deal with life, and in particular, its problems. How do you react? Do you give in, presuming that there is no hope; do you worry, do you panic, do you shy away and divert power into undesirable areas? In short, are you negative or positive? Always remember, "As you THINK—So you ARE."

The type of thinking that you generally apply toward life will always dictate what happens next. In other words, negative experiences arise when your dominant thoughts have a negative bias. The lesson is simply one of changing your thinking from negative to positive. This needs practice, but it is well worth the effort. Constantly look at yourself to see how you react, and each time you find that you are being negative, stop, remind yourself that your thinking will affect the outcome, then change your approach to positive. You will find that negative thinking is a "habit" that has crept into your life and only by adopting a new and better habit can you be rid of it. Dominant, negative thoughts are bound to impinge on your magical work, for they are part of you. By gradually ridding yourself of them, your magical work will improve enormously.

There are, however, other problems that directly affect your magical work. Some stem from habit, others are more subtle. On a deeper level, there are other problems that do not manifest until you are beginning to make progress. Effective magick is proportional not only to knowledge and expertise, but also in the ability to overcome these additional inner problems. I say "inner" because they exist deep within the subconscious mind and are usually unnoticed. Nevertheless, these barriers or blocks are very real. Until they are removed, they will constantly divert power into undesirable areas. These are the beliefs about yourself and your world that instruct the subconscious mind to set up situations that may be contrary to your conscious intent. They continue to function until altered. A classic example of this would be found in the magician who, having had some success, tries to attain greater things but who still has a deep-seated belief that success is "bad." The more the magician tries, the less successful he or she is. There seems to be some force working against this person, which there is. It would be easy to mistakenly blame karma, fate, or the intervention of some cosmic being while the problem lies within. Of course, anyone who knows the mechanism of magick will not subscribe to these silly ideas, yet many do, thereby substantiating what is already believed to be true. The net result: failure.

Magician—Know Thy Self!

So, what is to be done? The old idea of "Know Thy Self" is the key. If you wish to have greater power, then look at yourself, and in particular, your beliefs. Question these to see if they are valid and, more importantly, where you got them from in the first place. Your habits will also afford valuable clues as to what these inner problems are, and much can be done by changing bad habits. One of the best ways to enhance your life and to improve your magical work is to look at yourself and your habits and be perfectly honest with yourself. Once you realize you have a bad habit, offer yourself the logical argument that it is of no use, therefore you want to be rid of it. The moment you make a concerted effort to rid yourself of a bad habit, by systematic refusal to conform to the habit, you will eventually remove it from your being and remove the cause from your subconscious mind. The theory is quite valid and can easily be proved by anyone who has sufficient motivation and patience. In practice, however, it is not that easy. Old habits die hard. So, what is to be done? Embarking on a program of self-searching, through ritual procedures and deep meditation will help, because all things are proportional to effort. The real adept will sooner or later have to come to terms with the "self" by this, or a similar, process.

In order to remove bad habits you want to get together a plan of action based on sound principles and symbolism. The magical way to achieve success is to first have an intention that the subconscious mind will accept as an instruction. The intention is quite obvious—to get rid of a particular bad habit. How to gain the cooperation of your subconscious mind is another matter! The color of magick, or the four elements, may be used to act as a symbolic link, by using ritual procedures and by grouping habits according to the corresponding element or color and using these to target the problem.

Washing Your Ego Clean

Your first task will be to know yourself. Each initiation system, no matter which kind it may be, begins with this training. Without self-knowledge there can be no real development in magical training.

In the first days of your magical training, you should concern yourself with the practice of knowing your "good" (angelic) and "bad" (demonic) points. For this, you need to start a magical diary. Make a list of your bad points, so you can look at them. This diary is for your use only, and must not be shown to anyone else. In your search for your failures, bad habits, passions, instincts and other ugly character traits, you must take a long hard look at yourself. You may have to be a bit severe. Be merciless! Don't embellish or ameliorate any of your failures and deficiencies. Think about yourself in quiet meditation, put yourself back into different situations in your past; remember how you behaved and the kinds of mistakes and failures that took place in the various situations. Make notes of all your weaknesses, down to the finest nuisances and variations. The more you discover, the better for you. Nothing can stay hidden, nothing stays unrevealed, however insignificant or great your faults or frailties may be. Some people have been able to rediscover hundreds of failures in the finest shades. People like these possess good meditation skills and are able to penetrate deeply into their own ego. Wash your ego perfectly clean, sweep all the dust out of it.

This self-analysis is one of the most important magical preludes. Many mystical and magical systems have neglected it, and that is why they do not achieve good results. Self-analysis is indispensable to obtaining a magical equipoise, and without it, there is no regular progress of development. You probably will want to organize a regime and put aside some minutes for self-criticism in the morning and at night. If you have some free moments during the day, use them to do some intense thinking and remembering. Are there still some faults hidden anywhere? If you discover some, record them on the spot so you won't forget a single one! Whenever you happen to remember another deficiency, note it down immediately.

If, within a week, you do not succeed in discovering all your faults, spend another week on these inquiries until you have definitely established a list. Having achieved this task within one or two weeks, you are ready to begin the next exercise. Now, by intensive thinking, try to assign each fault to one of the four elements. Appoint a rubric, or title, in your magical notebook to each element and enter your faults under each one. It will be difficult to assign some faults to a particular element. Record these under the heading of "indifferent." As your development progresses, you will be able to determine the element corresponding to your deficiency. For example, you can ascribe your faults as follows:

1. AIR: Frivolity, self-presumption, boasting, squandering, gossiping;

2. FIRE: Jealousy, hatred, vindictiveness, irascibility, anger;

3. WATER: Indifference, frigidity, compliance, negligence, shyness, insolence, instability;

4. EARTH: Laziness, conscienceless, melancholy, irregularity, anomaly, and dullness.

In the following week, meditate on each single rubric, dividing it into three groups. In the first group, enter the biggest failings, especially those that influence you the most—or happen at the slightest opportunity. The second group will encompass faults occurring less frequently and in a lesser degree. In the last group, you should record those faults that happen only now and again. Categorize your indifferent faults in the three groups, as well. Work conscientiously at all times; it is worth while! Repeat the whole procedure with your good qualities, entering them into the respective categories of the elements. Do not forget the three columns here. So, for example, you assign the elements as follows:

1. AIR: Diligence, joy, dexterity, kindness, lust, optimism;
2. FIRE: Activity, enthusiasm, firmness, courage, daring;
3. WATER: Modesty, abstemiousness, fervency, compassion, tranquillity, tenderness, forgiveness;
4. EARTH: Respect, endurance, conscientiousness, thoroughness, sobriety, punctuality, responsibility.

By doing this, you will get two types of personal qualities—good and difficult character traits. You must endeavor to evaluate your ego precisely and conscientiously. If, in the course of your development, you remember any good or difficult quality, you can still record it under the appropriate heading. These two personal opposites will allow you, as a magician, to recognize exactly which elements are prevailing. This recognition is absolutely necessary to attain a magical equipoise, and further development depends on it.[3]

---

[3] A useful technique for influencing aspects of human behavior is self-hypnosis. See Leslie M. LeCron, *Self-Hypnosis: The Technique and Its Use in Daily Living* (New York: Signet, 1970).

3

MAGICAL
PRELIMINARIES

THIS CHAPTER DEALS WITH THE TEMPLE, the Magick Circle, and the Four Gateways of Power. A true Magick Circle is a symbol. Unless it exists in the imagination, it is of no use. Note that the temple and other pieces of magical equipment are only used to enhance the magical operation by giving the mind something to concentrate on. These things appeal to the intellect and to the emotions, helping the mind to focus on the task in hand. By all means, have a temple, robe, and equipment. They can only help. But remember that, without the right attitude of mind, none of these will serve any useful purpose, other than costing you time and money. Eventually, you can dispense with all of these if you wish.

The Temple and Magical Equipment

It is important to view the temple and equipment in the light of common sense. If you are fortunate enough to have a spare room that you can use as a permanent temple, well and good. This room ought to be designated as a temple and used for nothing else. Clear everything out and try to keep it as a special place. Do not fill it full of furniture and odds and ends. Take into your temple only the things you feel belong there. Start from nothing and build up gradually, avoiding clutter. Clean and decorate if you wish. I also suggest that you cover any windows to keep out prying eyes. The more light you exclude, the more effective the magical lighting you are going to use later on will be.[1] Put a strong lock on the door to keep out intruders.

The first rule of magick is to "Keep Silent." Keep your magick to yourself and those of a similar persuasion whom you can trust. If you have a cellar or an attic, so much the better. A permanent place can be a real advantage at first. If you don't have a spare room, be creative. A little improvisation may solve the problem. Sometimes it is necessary to accept second best, waiting patiently for the ideal to arrive. Although you may already have a mental picture of a temple with lots of space, it is far better to start small than not to start at all. After all, you can use this small start as a spur to better things, working magick to obtain a better temple.

If, after exhausting all the possibilities, there is nowhere to be found for a permanent temple, think in terms of a temporary one. You really need some place that you can go to work magick, even if you have to share with a friend or use the garden shed. A temporary temple is the answer to a lot of problems, so look around for some convenient place to work, even if this means moving a bit of furniture. Do not forget to clear away all the magical equipment when you have finished. Do not leave it lying around for all and sundry to stare at. There are still enough sadly misguided people around who will stop at nothing to prevent you from practicing the magical arts.

Having looked at the temple you may wish to acquire some additional equipment. This will repay you many times over. There is no need to spend a fortune on equipment, however. Let common sense be your guide.

---

[1] Subdued lighting from candles, oil lamps, or a rotary dimmer switch available from electrical appliance shops and stores.

The Altar

An altar is simply a convenient work surface. It can be made of anything you like and it can be any shape or size. Traditionalists may opt for the double-cube shape, as this contains much in the way of symbolism. When you have decided what to use, you must then convert it into an acceptable altar. It is a good idea to use an altar cloth in the correct color. Color should be worked into the ritual as much as possible. Candles, altar cloths, and robes made in inexpensive materials are all useful. Rather than have a wardrobe full of robes in various colors, make or purchase one robe in a neutral color and have different colored sashes or cords for each rite. Robes are useful, as they help the vital transition from real to magical time. There is no reason why you cannot work skyclad.[2]

Additional Equipment

When you have acquired a useful work surface, think about additional equipment. Be guided by this thought: All magical equipment must be symbolic and the symbolism must be understood. This simply means that each piece of equipment must represent an *idea*. It is a mistake to presume that magical equipment is effective by itself. It is not! The magick lies within you, in your mind. Anything that enhances this symbolic power is bound to be worthy of consideration. Therefore, choose your equipment carefully, so that it helps you to concentrate on the task in hand.

Take candles as an example. Naturally, you are going to need some form of lighting as an alternative to electric light. From this point of view alone, candles are a valuable ritual aid. Resist the temptation to pile these up on the altar. Think carefully first. How best will these serve your needs? How can you use them to maximum advantage?

---

[2] "Skyclad" is a Wicca term for working naked. You can, of course, wear whatever you feel to be specifically relevant, as long as it allows for physical freedom and is suitable.

I suggest that you start with a single candle placed in the center of your altar. Let this symbolize the inner power of your subconscious mind, rather than using it simply as a source of light. Already there is a difference, because you have changed your *attitude* toward the light. The relationship between you and the candle has changed subtly—your association with it has altered. No longer is it a plain candle. It is a symbolic light. On the surface, nothing has changed. There is, however, a change within your mind and, as you now know, magick is the science of using your mind. If this were an ordinary candle, you would simply light it without a second thought. With a symbolic candle, the approach is bound to be different, owing to a change in your attitude. In this example, the candle represents your inner power, so deal with it in this context. When you light it, your inner power is *on,* and you are in contact with it. When extinguished, everything returns to normal. By building up associations in this way, an ordinary candle becomes magical in the truest sense of word.

If you wish to add more candles, do so. Always remember that they must symbolize something, whether this be inner power or external energy. Color can be used to good effect if you bear in mind that it is not the color itself that causes power to flow, but the associations made in your mind. A good example of this is the use of green in money rituals.[3]

Sun/Moon Centering, the Cosmic Sphere, and the Four Gateways of Power

Not many people are aware of the fact that a magical ritual is simply a means of focusing the mind along a specific channel. The purpose of a ritual is simply to bring together all those things that are likely to aid this focus, so that your subconscious mind may be influenced according to your needs. As such, there is nothing wrong with ritual, provided that it does

---

[3] The colors of magick are fully discussed in Part II of this book, The Psybernomicon.

not descend to the worship of various entities. The components of a ritual are:

1. The all-important intention of the rite.
2. Pre-ritual relaxation (use the Sun/Moon centering if you so desire). Do not think about the rite. This should be done before you start. When ready, move to the center of the temple and become quiet, thinking only that "something" is about to happen.
3. Performance of the ritual.
4. The high-point of the ritual—performing the main magical work.
5. Returning to everyday matters.

If you are using a ritual to influence your subconscious mind, you must do it in an effective way. As part of this process, gradually build up in your mind symbolism that your subconscious understands. Put simply, it is of no use to say to your subconscious mind: "Now look here, I want you to give me some power to bring about—whatever." The basic idea may be correct, but the approach is unworkable because your subconscious does not understand words, whether English, Greek, Hebrew, Enochian, or Latin. No, you have to find a better way. You must look at what you are trying to achieve.

The following exercises are important from two points of view. First, they will help you relax and push away distracting thoughts. Second, they are potent symbols that your subconscious mind fully understands. They are divided into three stages for convenience.

Stage One: Sun/Moon Centering

This is suitable for removing feelings of "impurity" (especially prior to a ritual). Stand at attention and take a few minutes to quiet your mind. Visualize either a brilliant, pearly Moon-sphere, or an incandescent solar disc glowing or shining above your head. As you breathe in, begin to draw the

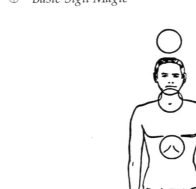

Figure 1. Sun/Moon centering.

Sun/Moon down. It will pass slowly, very slowly, through your body with each inhalation, filling you with a pure, clean radiance. When it has passed completely through your body and into the floor, reverse the process and raise the light disc up again through your body, this time with each exhalation (this is optional), until it shines once more above your head. You may pay particular attention to any part of your body that needs this healing or cleansing (see figure 1 above).

Stage Two: The Cosmic Sphere—How to Open and Close a Ritual

Your subconscious mind is capable of anything. All that you have to do is communicate in a rational manner to get it to do anything. First, however, you must inform it that you are about to issue an instruction. This is important, because you have to get around the natural safety mechanism that prevents normal, everyday thoughts from influencing the subconscious mind. In short, you need a magical on/off switch. This is accomplished by using an opening and closing formula.

There are many of these and, although the basic procedure and structure is essentially the same, you should construct your own so that it becomes personal. Your opening formula needs to be symbolic, because your subconscious mind deals with symbols.

By far the best symbol is that of the Encircled Cross. This is the master symbol from which all others are derived. Most of you will be familiar with the Magick Circle. This is a parody of the Encircled Cross symbol (see figure 2, page 30). The true Magick Circle exists in your mind. It is not flat; it is three-dimensional. This is where most mistakes are made. The Encircled Cross, when viewed from above a Magick Circle, is in reality, a sphere—a cosmic sphere in which you work. To construct this in your mind is quite easy, but it does require some practice. The results, however, are well worth the effort.

Start by imagining a point of light within yourself at about heart level. This symbolizes your inner subconscious power. Then form your arms into the cross. Imagine that a beam of light travels from your center, vertically upward, terminating above your head as a symbol of a crown. A similar beam of light now travels vertically downward, terminating below your feet as a symbol of a cubic black stone. The vertical axis is complete. Keeping the idea of beams of light traveling from your center, imagine that one now travels out in front of you, terminating in the symbol of a Sword. This direction is known as magical east. Move your attention to your right and see another beam radiate outward to become a symbol of a Wand or spear at magical south. Behind you now radiates a beam that terminates as the symbol of the Cup or chalice at magical west. Finally, an arm travels out to your left, terminating as the symbol of the shield at magical north.

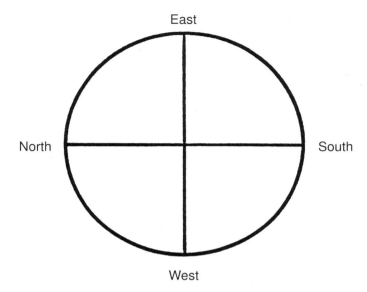

Figure 2. The Encircled Cross.

The six arms of the Encircled Cross are now complete. All that remains is to add the circles to complete the Cosmic Sphere. Starting at the crown above your head, imagine a circle of light traveling to the right, through the cube at your feet, then to the left and back to the crown. A second beam starts at the front, magical east, and moves in a clockwise direction through south, west, north and back to east again. The final circle starts at the top and travels through front, base, rear, and back to the top. You now have a Cosmic Sphere containing a center, six arms radiating out toward the appropriate symbols, and three rings connecting these arms (see figure 3, page 31).

This formula may easily be ritualized by using gestures and words, provided that you use your imagination while doing this. It is the imagination that influences the subconscious, not words. Naturally, you may think up your own, but here is a suggestion.

It is useful to understand the symbolism of different parts of the Cosmic Sphere. The crown symbolizes power, and it is

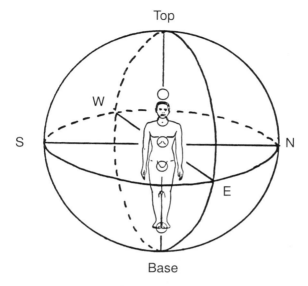

Figure 3. The Cosmic Sphere.

from here that power emanates into the four magical directions. Power flows out from the crown, through the arms of the sphere, to perform the task you have instructed it to do.

The arms of the sphere represent the four magical elements in their respective colors: the element Air and the color yellow; the element Fire and the color red; the element Water and the color blue; and the element Earth and the color green. It is through these elements that the power of the crown flows into the world to create change.

Power that has been sent forth always returns. The power that you send out from the crown through the elements returns to the cubic black stone at the feet. Here, the power comes to rest and germinates. Here, the intention of the mind and the power bring your magical work to fruition.

There are many ramifications in the relationship of the parts of the Cosmic Sphere. This brief discussion is by no means exhaustive, but it does provide a basic framework for the beginning practitioner. The power of the crown is upward, creation through the four elements is outward, and all comes to rest and fruition in the cubic black stone.

The Cosmic Sphere
Opening Formula

Center yourself using the Sun/Moon centering ritual and then perform the following formula, saying:

"From the infinite power of my inner silent center do I construct my inner cosmos."

[Visualize the central point.]

"I am connected to the potential of the All-Father principle."

[Visualize the crown.]

"I am equally connected to the principle of the Earth-Mother."

[Visualize the cube.]

"Around me are the four symbols of dynamic power. Before me lies the symbol of perfect intelligence and awareness."

[Visualize the Sword.]

"To my right lies the symbol of perfect creativity."

[Visualize the Wand.]

"Behind me lies the symbol of eternal outpouring goodness."

[Visualize the Cup.]

"To my left lies the symbol of my being."

[Visualize the shield.]

"One is the totality of existence."

[Visualize the first ring.]

"Two is the reality of potential."

[Visualize the second ring.]

"Three is the number of power."

[Visualize the third ring.]

"From center to circumference, all is connected according to cosmic law. Be this Cosmic Sphere declared open."

Magical work may now begin. When you are finished, you must close down this Cosmic Sphere before returning to normal time and space. This is done by simply reversing the procedure. A suggestion for suitable wording follows.

Closing Formula

Say:

"Let there be peace to the highest."

[See the crown disappear.]

"Let there be peace to the lowest."

[See the cube disappear.]

"Let there be peace to the east."

[See the Sword disappear.]

"Let there be peace to the south."

[See the Wand disappear.]

"Let there be peace to the west."

[See the Cup disappear.]

"Let there be peace to the north."

[See the shield disappear.]

"Let there be peace all around."

[See the rings disappear.]

"Let there be peace within."

[See the light at the center disappear.]

"I now declare this ritual complete and this Cosmic Sphere returned to normality."

With practice, the process of erecting the Cosmic Sphere will become second nature. As it does, the time spent on this may be reduced. The whole point of magick is to be quick, effective, and simple. Long rituals are necessary in the early stages simply to educate your mind. With the passing of time and a subsequent increase in confidence, techniques should be speeded up, in the same way that a would-be pianist, having mastered the scales, then starts to play fluently.

Each of the four elements has a corresponding magical weapon—Air/Sword, Fire/Wand, Water/Cup, and Earth/Magical Shield. There is no need to actually possess the magical weapon. It is your inner understanding of the weapons that matters, your inner imaginative linkage. The aim of the true magician is to link, within the self, the greater and lesser natures. To do this many have used symbolic weapons to bridge the gap between physicality and mentality. The four principal weapons are symbolic of the elements of Air, Fire, Water, and Earth.

The Sword (Air): The Sword represents the creative will and the intelligence. It represents the ability to conceive an idea and bring it to reality in action.

The Wand (Fire): Its image is the same as that of Fire. It disperses material things into gases and residues. The Wand or spear generally inspires respect and implies authority and desire.

The Cup (Water): The magical cup presents the essence of life, the overflowing of divine love. The Cup or chalice refreshes, rejuvenates, revitalizes. It is the divine mother, the grand lady of nature. The Cup is supplication, humility, and emotions.

The Magical Shield (Earth): The Magical Shield represents inert matter, the material world, with all its hardships and struggles. It is the darkest state of being. Its use is to represent ethereal qualities upon the material plane. It is analogous to salt, which preserves flesh and thus material existence. The finished object.

Thus, in short:

> With the Sword createth thee.
> With the Wand destroyeth thee.
> With the Cup nourisheth thee.
> With the Shield preserveth thee.

Stage Three: The Four Gateways of Power

Become calm, then perform the Sun/Moon centering and open the Cosmic Sphere as described. Now imagine that, at each of the four points, there is a doorway that can be opened or closed at will. Through these symbolic doorways flows life energy that can be directed to obtain the results you desire. Treat this exercise seriously and spend some time using your imagination to see these doorways opening and closing at your command. It is often a good idea to use simple phrases as key words, or "sacred words," as they are sometimes called. As a suggestion try: "Let the portals be opened." To close, use: "Let the portals be closed." Naturally, you may use whatever wording you desire. There is no need to use my words. At conclusion of this exercise, close the Cosmic Sphere as before.

The exercise just given should not be rushed or treated as pointless. Remember that you are dealing with your mind, and that your mind is a tool. With practice, your subconscious will obey your visualization and realize that you are taking control of this power. As with any skill involving the use of tools, patience and practice is needed to obtain the best results.

The final stage of this exercise should also be practiced carefully. It is here that you will conjure with this magical ritual framework. Relax, clear your mind using the Sun/Moon centering, then open the Cosmic Sphere. Either out loud or silently in your mind, use the conjurations, bringing in the extra dimension of the symbolic doorways as follows:

Center yourself and say:

"In the first instance, there is life energy, constantly outpouring, without beginning or end. It is abundant and is designed to be used creatively."

[Imagine that the eastern doorway now opens, allowing yellow energy to pour through. Use a command phrase if desired. Remember that the eastern doorway is in front of you.] Say:

"In the second instance, there is my subconscious mind, which acts as a mediator for life energy. It is my servant and seeks only to assist and to answer questions truthfully. It knows no limits other than those I choose to define. It can and does affect circumstances, events, and physical matter in accordance with the instructions I give it. It will, therefore, never fail me."

[Imagine that the southern doorway opens, allowing red energy to pour through.] Say:

"In the third instance, there is my will to determine what the future should or should not be and the absolute truth of free choice. Therefore, I am bound by no beliefs other than those I choose to adopt."

[Imagine that the western doorway now opens, allowing blue energy to pour through.] Say:

In the fourth instance, there is physical matter, which is enlivened and given form by life energies. By free choice and with the aid of my subconscious mind, matter must respond to my will."

[Imagine that the northern doorway now opens, allowing green energy to pour through.]

With practice, this exercise provides a perfect framework for performing rituals and casting sigil spells for whatever workings you may choose. The amount of time spent is entirely up to you. There are no hard and fast rules, so let your own feelings and inclinations be your guide. The only rule of thumb is not to rush through these exercises. Magical success is governed by the simple measure, input = output. In short, you only get out in direct proportion to what you put in. This has nothing to do with money, but it has everything to do with personal involvement and the small sacrifice of time and effort needed to gain results.

It is important to remember that you need to be able to carry magical awareness around with you. It is not sufficient to be a Saturday-night magician. Avoid the absurdity—and I have seen this happen—of people who, suddenly faced with a problem, think that because they have not got their robes, incense, temple, or even lodge members, they just cannot function. I have seen entire lodges grind to a halt because someone did not turn up. This hardly makes things practical.

The dynamic, fourfold pattern of power can be carried around in your imagination anywhere. Furthermore, it can be used, because all you have to do is erect the Cosmic Sphere in your mind, as described. Then, by opening the four gateways of power in your imagination and thinking creatively, all manner of everyday things start to get done. Work with it, get to know it, and make it very familiar to yourself. It will repay you many times over.

If words are used, they work because you put feelings, belief, and imagination into them. For instance, if you are facing a particular quarter and simply say, "I declare this quarter open," it is one thing to say or vibrate those words and not think about them, but it is another to see vividly in your imagination that that doorway opens up releasing colored energy. By using feeling and imagination with your words you can work absolute wonders. The words, whatever they are, then become vehicles that express emotion and imagination. There is a world of difference.

I recommend performing the Sun/Moon-disc centering, the Cosmic Sphere, and Four Gateways of Power exercises on a regular basis, even if you are not performing any specific magical operation. This keeps things ticking over, so to speak, and serves for magical protection, creating a physical and spiritual equilibrium for security and assertiveness. The precept "invoke often" reveals its importance here.

You may wonder how it is possible to see the Cosmic Sphere in your mind's eye, while imagining it and also imagining the four gateways. In other words, how do you imagine two things at once. It is all a question of memory. Let me explain.

To imagine several different things all at the same time would, of course, be difficult, if not impossible. Fortunately, you do not need to do this. As you build up the Cosmic Sphere, you establish each part of it in your memory, moving on through each successive stage and concentrating only on whatever is necessary. For instance, you start with the central light, imagining that this exists. Then, your attention moves on to the next stage of imagining the first of the six arms. There is no need to keep the image of the central light constantly in your imagination, because it is presumed to exist and, in fact, does exist in your memory. You use this and similar procedures in everyday life. For example, suppose you were standing in a room facing a window. You see the window quite clearly. If you turn round to face the opposite wall, you of course, see the wall instead. You still know, however, that the window exists because you have just seen it. In fact, you can recall this in your imagination, because the image is stored in your memory. In a similar fashion, having become familiar with the room, you "know" what the room looks like in totality without actually seeing it physically.

It is exactly the same with the Cosmic Sphere and inner "seeing." In other words, use your imagination to build up an imaginary sphere in your memory. All through the building-up procedure, you establish each stage before moving on to the next. Therefore, at the high-point of the ritual, you are free to concentrate fully on the work at hand, knowing that the Cosmic Sphere exists in your memory, because you have put it there.

At the end of the ritual, you must inform your subconscious that the sphere and gateways are no longer established, hence the need for a closing procedure. Never forget that, although the Cosmic Sphere and the gateways are imaginary and it would be easy to dismiss the entire concept as worthless, this is not the case. Any deliberate erection of a symbolic pattern will have an effect on your subconscious, because you are using what is, in effect, a powerful language that the subconscious understands. It is, therefore, necessary to treat these symbols with respect and practice using them often. You should also bear in mind that symbols are not holy or sacred, so to worship them is sheer folly. Likewise, they are not meant to be worn as ornaments or lucky charms. People who do so show a marked lack of understanding as to the real nature of symbols.

4

CREATING SIGILS

THE SECRETS OF REAL MAGICK LIE IN UNDERSTANDING your subconscious mind. This incredible part of you is limitless, totally creative, and all-knowing. Never underestimate its capabilities, or the fact that you are able to control and direct it as you will. All miracles and so-called paranormal happenings are due to the workings of the subconscious mind. It is also responsible for many feats that cannot be explained by science. When given an instruction, it will always carry this out, no matter what the facts appear to be. How? The answer is *connection*.

Subconscious Universal Energy, Universal Intelligence and Universal Mind

Your subconscious mind has access to the abundant power that exists everywhere in creation. It can, at any time, draw on this power and direct it toward some objective. There are no restrictions on the availability of power or on its use.

Universal intelligence (God) is totally cooperative and all-knowing. Your subconscious mind is in direct contact with this at all times. Every help will be given and all questions answered if you ask, for God is there to help. It is so very important that you examine your beliefs about divinity and then remove all concepts that are not valid or true. Wrong beliefs produce wrong results every time. If your God appears to hate you, it is because you believe this to be true, even though it is not! Remember that no god seeks to restrict or deprive you, or to make you pay for your supposed sins. These ideas are the legacy of the Dark Ages, when narrow-minded religions were the norm. The unthinking bigots and blind fools who fostered these idiotic schemes for their own purposes are still with us today. Do not listen to them. Instead, think about this carefully and come to your own conclusions. Open up to the reality of God and to the fact that this intelligence seeks only to help you have whatever you wish. God contact transforms lives by giving freedom—not by seeking to control and direct you. By abandoning self-restrictive ideas about universal intelligence, you automatically open up channels to power that will astound you.

By virtue of connection, you have access to power and knowledge. There are, however, many other levels and dimensions within the subconscious mind. If you consider the fact that everyone has a subconscious mind, it naturally follows that we are all connected to power and creative intelligence. We are also connected to each other. Many extraordinary phenomena can be explained by this linkage. For instance, nothing is forgotten. Nothing is ever forgotten by your subconscious, it retains everything. You cannot really forget something. The problem is simply one of not being able to recall something from memory. The idea of total retention is confirmed by hypnosis, under which a person can regress back to childhood and vividly experience some long-forgotten event as though it were real. Memory has many branches. One of these carries the total impressions of everyone who happens to be related by blood. In other words, you have inherited the memories of all those who went before.

Perhaps the most important link is the one you have with everyone else—not only those who are alive, here and now, but also those who are no longer incarnate. This does not mean that you are still in contact. Aunt Hilda will not come back from beyond the grave. All that is implied is that you are able to contact (and experience) the past impressions of someone else. To believe that these impressions are yours is sheer folly. Think about this carefully. Do you really wish to subscribe to the highly dubious concept of reincarnation, or the even sillier dogma of karma, or can you now see how these recollections are actually occurring through the linkages made by your subconscious mind? There cannot be any such thing as enforced Earth life, in which we serve out some sentence, paying for past mistakes of which we are not even aware. The whole concept is absurd and in direct opposition to common sense and truth.

The linkage between yourself and everyone else is called universal mind. Forget about superstitious claptrap concerning this. The universal mind is, quite simply, a perfectly natural linkage on subconscious levels. It gives you free access to many wonders, experiences, and memories. It also gives you the total cooperation of every living being in creation, because subconscious minds cannot, by themselves, say no. Here is the great oneness—the universal brother- and sisterhood of humanity. Those who learn to rise above normal human failings and contact the universal mind, will inevitably gain the complete cooperation of all others. The key, once again, lies in your beliefs.

Symbols

The key to the subconscious, especially from a magical point of view, lies in the use of symbols. Any valid symbol acts as a doorway between you and this powerful part of your mind. It is the key that unlocks the door to power and knowledge if used correctly. Let us now explore symbols or, to be more precise, sigils, and see where it leads us.

This basic method was developed by the artist and magician Austin Osman Spare during the early part of the 20th century. In my opinion, Spare was a greater contributor to the world of magick than his contemporary and mentor, Aleister Crowley.[1] Spare was a visionary artist of considerable talent, notable for many other things outside magick. He received a national award for mathematics and was the youngest person ever to exhibit at the National Gallery.[2] Spare knew both Aleister Crowley and Gerald Gardner, but himself shunned ceremonial styles (both the high magical style of Crowley and the coven rites of Gardner's Wicca).[3] Instead, he developed a paradigm based on very simple principles. He bequeathed to us a refinement of sigilization—a process of true primal magick for realizing desires. This was just one element of the highly individualistic philosophy that Spare called "Zos Kia Cultus."[4]

Sigilization, although derived from within a ceremonial paradigm, can be performed without complex ritual regalia and exacting periods of preparation. Sigils can be applied equally well to changing anything from the weather to some internal situation (for example, to come to terms with your anger or to spark inspiration for a specific project). There are two approaches to be considered: graphic sigils and mantric sigils.

Basic Concepts

Sigils are images that unconsciously represent your desire. The aim of sigilization is to create an image (usually a symbol of some type) that represents your magical intention. The image is made in such a way that your conscious mind will

---

[1] Aleister Crowley, "The Great Beast 666," who initiated a new aeon of spirituality in 1904, supposedly through communication with a discarnate entity, Aiwaz. Thelemic magick is largely the legacy of Mr. Crowley.

[2] Austin Osman Spare, *From the Inferno to Zos: The Writings and Images of Austin Osman Spare,* vol 1. (Seattle, WA: Holmes, 1993); Vera Wainwright, *Poems and Masks* (London: Mandrake, 1991).

[3] Gerald B. Gardner, founder of what came to be known as the Gardnerian Tradition of Witchcraft, is best remembered as the individual chiefly responsible for the Witchcraft revival in the modern West.

[4] Kenneth Grant, *Images and Oracles of Austin Osman Spare* (London: Frederick Muller, 1975), p. 7.

not make an immediate connection between it and the object of your desire.

Sigils work by exploiting a fundamental difference in the way the conscious and subconscious minds operate. They operate at a point halfway between the conscious and subconscious levels. A sigil is composed of letters (the language of the conscious mind) formed into a pattern (the symbol-speak of the subconscious mind). In this way a sigil allows the conscious desire to enter the subconscious mind, where it can tap into the powerhouse of magick. Sigils hover between the two realms, opening a channel between the rational, logical mind of mundane reality and the symbolic, magical realm of the subconscious. When a sigil has thus been cast, it is then forgotten. Forgetting what you just did can often be the hardest part of the process. Magick works when the subconscious is left alone to do its job. The sigil floats away from conscious awareness and into the depths of the subconscious. As long as you do not dwell on the intention whenever it pops up into normal consciousness—a problem termed "lust of result"—it should not matter too much. In other words, you need to forget what you want in order for the subconscious to get to work on your desire.

Creating Graphic Sigils

Write out your intention in capitals. The simplest and most commonly used paradigm to create a sigil is the classic method described by Spare.[5] Alternatively, you can try this slightly easier method, which uses the same principles. First, decide what you want. Depending on your own magical belief system, your views on karma and so forth, you may want to spend some time considering carefully how to word your sigil spell. Before proceeding it is important to get a clear, well-thought-out intention into your mind—one with which you feel both emotionally and intellectually happy.

---

[5] Spare, *From the Inferno to Zos: The Writings and Images of Austin Osman Spare*, p. 50.

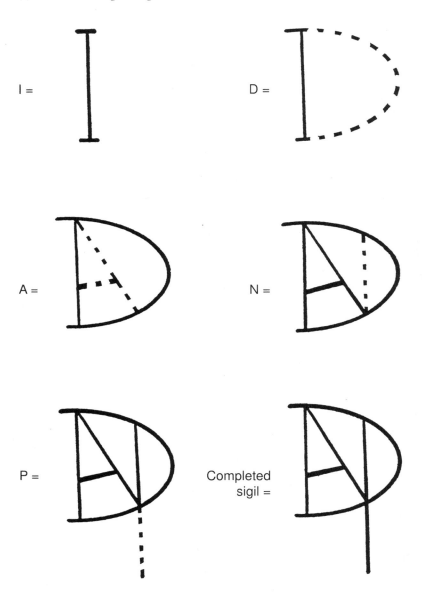

I =

D =

A =

N =

P =

Completed
sigil =

Figure 4. Constructing sigils.

Figure 5. A decorated sigil.

Having established what you want, write down this desire in capital letters as one simple statement. For instance: **I DESIRE A NEW PARTNER.**[6] Then use the first letter of each word, removing any letters that are repeated. Thus, the example given becomes: I   D   A   N   P.

Experiment with the letter forms that remain, overlaying one on top of another until you arrive at the sigil. This will be a shape with which you are aesthetically happy, one that contains within itself all the first letters from your original statement of desire, as in the example shown in figure 4 (page 44). It is permissible to consider M as a reversed W or, seen from the side, as an E. Therefore, these three letters do not have to appear in the sigil three separate times.

It does not matter what the sigil looks like as long as it is not too complex. All you need is a simple symbol on which to focus your attention. You must be able to visualize it (hold it firmly in the imagination throughout the ritual) and it must look right, according to your intuition. Decorating sigils can

---

[6] It is generally unwise to cast spells for the attraction of specific partners. It is better to conjure for suitable partners in general, for yourself or others. Your subconscious usually has a far more subtle appreciation of who really is suitable.

help by making them look even more magical (see figure 5, page 45). Stylizing the sigil with magical embroideries and decoration may seem romantic and whimsical, but this can enhance its effect tremendously. In figure 6, I have taken this idea even further by giving the sigil a Gothic style that can help to facilitate the arousal of subconscious activity and primordial impulses to liberate the magical power within (see below). The refined sigil will appear to the subconscious as more magical, because it differs from our smoothed-up plastic everyday niceties and pseudo-aesthetics.

As a final thought, you may wish to place a border around the sigil, in the form of a triangle, circle, square, or something similar. This is entirely up to you.

When you are satisfied with your sigil, draw it on a piece of paper. You will need to transform it from a mere doodle into a magically potent image. To do this, you will need to charge the sigil using some form of magical gnosis and sleight-of-mind procedure. Charging methods are fully discussed in chapters 5 and 15.

Figure 6. Gothic "rough-hewn" style.

Creating Mantric Sigils

Write out your intention. You can spell it phonetically or scramble it into a meaningless phrase or a word that is pleasant to your ear. This can then be chanted throughout the ritual. You may add some vowels to make vocalization easier.

Spinning Mantra

The spinning mantra places the emphasis on the second and fourth syllables of each line. The rhythm, speed, and excitement of this kind of mantra have a direct effect on the thought process. You will have to practice the mantra for a period of time before it can be used ritually. If you do not want to use the spinning mantra, simply chant the mantra so that it sounds euphonic as well as, somehow, magical.

Create a sentence of desire: I DESIRE A NEW PARTNER.

Spell the sentence phonetically: I DEZIAR A NU PARTNA.

Delete all repeated letters: I DEZAR NU PT.

Scramble and rearrange the letters to form a mantric spell: ZEID RAN TUP.

Next you must charge your sigil. You may already have a preferred way of doing this, but for those with less experience, I will explain in chapter 5 one method that can be used by those who prefer an excitatory ritualistic approach.

5

WHIRLING GNOSIS

MAGICK IS THE ART OF INFLUENCING the subconscious mind in order to gain information or obtain physical results. There are many methods that give the magician access to the subconscious using sleight-of-mind techniques. Within the paradigms contained in this book, I will call this gnosis. This means that the conscious mind can be raised to a high pitch, or gradually silenced, allowing the magical part of the mind to be contacted. There are many varied routes to achieving gnosis.

Magical Gnosis

Gnosis is the Greek word for "knowledge" or "means of knowing." It is used particularly in an esoteric sense. In the pragmatic interpretation, it is applied as much to a straightforward intellectual investigation as to any paradigm of consciousness modification or direct experience.

Among present-day magical practitioners, there is some consensus that the inducement of a state of gnosis is an essential prerequisite for any useful magical activity, be it divination, evocation, invocation, or simple spell casting. In this chapter, we will examine a number of techniques by which such a modified state of consciousness may be induced. As mentioned earlier, these can be divided into two broad categories: "inhibitory gnosis" (Hermetic Magick) and "excitatory gnosis" (Orphic Magick). Ultimately, I will focus on one technique, that of "whirling" to induce a gnostic state.

Inhibitory Gnosis

Inhibitory techniques are generally contemplative or yogic in character and are aimed at reducing sensory stimulus. In inhibitory gnosis, consciousness is subsumed, as in measured hypnotic conjuration.[1]

Excitatory Gnosis

Excitatory techniques, in contrast, depend on hyperstimulation as a means of modifying consciousness. This mode favors extremes or persistence with some energetic physical activity (such as a whirling dervish dance or the emotionally stimulating abandonment of circle dancing). Carried to the point of exhaustion, these can be effective, but sexual climax, as the ultimate expression of life, represents the pinnacle of excitatory gnosis.

Even though there is an apparent dichotomy between inhibitory and excitatory techniques, they achieve similar results. Both methods imprint the subconscious mind with a desired intention or release a specific suppressed component of the personality to be cathected or controlled.

The art and science of magick is a powerful psychodynamic system, even in an exclusively subjective or objective, phenomenologically conservative sense. The practice of magick is not as dangerous as credulous Christian critics contend, but neither is it frivolously dysfunctional as psychologists would suppose. In magick however, most magical transitive operations

---

[1] An example of how to use measured hypnotic conjuration, better known as measured gnostic conjuration, is given in chapter 15.

tend to fail because the aspiring magician does not understand the gnostic nature of the art.

Naturally, a little practice is in order before gnosis can be utilized in a ritual situation. A good deal of magical practice, therefore, revolves around developing the ability to enter gnosis and perhaps in some cases, to recognize it. Gnosis is generally understood to be the "peak" moment of any trance-inducing exercise wherein desire may be successfully phenomenized. The material, physical universe is, of necessity, a finite space. Gnosis will propel the magician, momentarily, beyond its confines. By this definition, anyone who is really concentrating on something, like reading a book or even watching television, may be said to be in gnosis or a trance of sorts. I am sure that most people are familiar with the freeway driving trance. Musical trances, especially drumming, displacement trances using dancing, and whirling dervish dances pursued to the point of exhaustion can all be effective along with other energetic physical activity. There are even general everyday trances. Trances are different and they have different levels of intensity and sensory selection.

Certain forms of inhibitory gnosis were known and used in ancient Egypt, where magician-priests officiated at secret temples in which sufferers of various afflictions were cured by invocation during visitations of the gods—most probably while the patients were in a somnambulistic trance. The ancient Greeks used similar practices, in which patients slept in the temple of Asclepius hoping for a dream-cure from the god.[2]

The Psychic Censor or Ego Filter

The ego level or censor is a filter that prevents the totality of information held in the subconscious from overwhelming the conscious mind. It also acts as a bridge that permits creative thinking to be impressed into the subconscious mind. When the ego filter or screen becomes soft and easy to penetrate,

---

[2] Ann Faraday, *The Dream Game* (New York: HarperPerennial, 1976), p. 63.

you can impress your desires upon the subconscious mind using symbolism. Before going any further, I want to dispel the idea that magical gnosis implies a similarity to the post-hypnotic demonstrations of the stage hypnotist. If that concept applied, a magician could hypnotize the subject and then instruct them (as in the following analogy) to see some spirit or god-force in the Triangle of Art[3] when the magician says the "key word," Abracadabra! Granted, such a procedure would probably work and might have some value in an experimental sense, but it is not the way that magick is practiced. This is a gimmicky approach at best, and, at worst, it can raise serious ethical questions.

To be able to shift your awareness or perspective at will from a hypothetical normal consciousness to a hypothetical magical consciousness is the trademark, test, and *raison d'être* of the genuine magician. Every individual will, and must, have a personal way of keying-in to altered states of awareness, otherwise termed magical gnosis. This can only be achieved through experimentation and practice using some form of ritual paradigm to induce a magical trance. Ritual magick is a valid art, not a psuedo-science. I define the magical trance as a state of heightened or subdued suggestibility in which the mind is totally centered on one idea or intention to the exclusion of everything else, including sensory perceptions that are unwanted or distracting.

---

[3] Sometimes a circle is used in ceremonial magick operations to summon visions of spirits, god-forces, and other entities, which are actually archetypes evoked from the deep mind via magical trance induction. The magicians of old tended to be more reactionary and superstitious—especially with their strongly Christian attitudes—and suspected that anything other than God was likely to be dangerous if summoned into the material world. They did not understand the operative technique, or had forgotten the essential principles of the art, and overlooked or co-opted its origins. These magicians used the Triangle of Art, as well as the magick circle, as an additional protective device to give them support. The magical instructions nearly always implied that you were likely to be dragged off to hell in an instant if anything went wrong!

Aleister Crowley defined magick as "The Science and Art of causing change in accordance with the will."[4] I'm defining it as the science and art of causing changes in consciousness to occur in magical operation in accordance with the will. The emphasis is on a change of consciousness or magical trance of sorts. Remember: magick is the art of causing changes in consciousness to occur in accordance with the will.

Having established that ritual magick needs some form of altered state of consciousness to be effective, we are ready to consider practical application and techniques.

The Whirling Magician—A Ritual Paradigm

Write out your intention or wish and form it into a graphic sigil. Spend several days concentrating on its form, so that you can easily hold it in your imagination. Prepare your temple and altar. Incense and a bit of drumming can also assist, but is best done somewhere where you are not likely to provoke an interruption.[5]

After a suitable period of calmness, approach the altar and light the central candle. This can be the color of the power being conjured. Place your sigil on the altar so it is visible to you from every part of the temple. Erect the Cosmic Sphere (see page 32), and open the ritual space, invoking the four gateways. Conjure the appropriate power, systematically, through each of the four doorways (see page 35). Initially, this should be done using the four doorways that equate to the four elements, which is the way in which power symbolically enters the theater of operations. There are points in this ritual at which each quarter is addressed. At each point, the doorway is opened and the power allowed in, finally impinging in the center of your own magical universe. At conclusion, reverse the procedure.

---

[4] Rodney Orpheus, *Abrahadabra: A Beginner's Guide to Thelemic Magick* (Stockholm: Looking Glass Press, 1995), p. 5.

[5] See Part II, The Psybernomicon, for this information.

Charging Methods

In order to preoccupy your conscious mind, you can use two methods simultaneously, drumming and whirling.[6] Modern recording and playback equipment affords many opportunities to bring sound into the temple, particularly drumming at the correct tempo. Prerecord a drumming tape, leaving the first part of it silent to enable you to erect the Cosmic Sphere and the four doorways. You can also use incantations using a sigilized mantra made from your desire sentence. This can be combined with the drumming and whirling dance by chanting it throughout the ritual. It, naturally, will take a little practice, especially the whirling, before all three methods can be utilized in a ritual paradigm. Both sonics and, in particular, the correct incense should be worked into the ritual. Incense is used as an aid to concentration and as a key to a particular level of consciousness. Sonics may be classified as out-sound and in-sound made by singing, or what is termed "vibrating," a word, verse, or divine name in a ritual. These can be linguistic or nonlinguistic utterances. A ritual sonic is more than just sound and is used rhythmically and intentionally to create a magical atmosphere, combined with incense, ritual paraphernalia, meditation music and/or drumming.

When the drumming starts, begin to whirl, building up speed gradually, until your arms begin to rise by the force generated and a rhythm is established. Maintain the speed throughout the ritual. Begin to chant the mantra and hold the sigil firmly in your imagination throughout the entire ritual.[7]

---

[6] Shamanistic drumming tapes are ideal as a musical background. My favorite piece is titled: "Drumming for the Shamanic Journey," an audio cassette tape distributed by The Foundation for Shamanic Studies, Box 1939, Mill Valley, CA 94942. Write to this address for this and other tapes. (I advise that anyone with epileptic tendencies avoid using drumming tapes.)

[7] The likely duration of the whirling is subject to the effect created by the lighting, incense, and music/drumming. Also, the time period can be anything from thirty minutes to one hour. Experiment yourself, starting with ten minutes and gradually extending this as you gain experience.

After a period of whirling, your conscious mind closes down and leaves a channel direct to your subconscious. Putting it another way, momentary suspensions of the conscious mind occur at points in the experience of whirling. It acts as a bridge that permits sigils to be encoded in the subconscious mind.[8]

As soon as you believe that the sigil has been imprinted on your subconscious mind, stop whirling, not suddenly, but slowly, to avoid becoming giddy. When you have stopped and recovered equilibrium, destroy the sigil or prepare it for disposal. For instance in summer it can be burnt, in spring it can be ripped and scattered to the four winds. In autumn, throw it into a river or plunge it into a bowl of water. In winter, bury it in a bowl of earth prior to burying it outside. Use whatever you feel to be correct for you. Your imagination and a little ingenuity will supply answers.

Return to normal by closing the four doorways in reverse order, and then allowing them to fade from view. Finally, close the Cosmic Sphere in the customary fashion and think no more of it.

Gone, but Not Forgotten

Gone, but not forgotten, is *not* the way of sigil magick. Whatever method you use to empower your sigil, once it has been emblazoned on your subconscious mind, it should be destroyed. This act is actually the most important part of the process. By destroying the sigil (which may be done in any number of ways, as already suggested) your desire is forgotten.

Learning to Forget

Forgetting what you want to happen is vitally important. Magick works best when the subconscious mind is left to its own devices

---

[8] Here is another technique you can try. It is fairly simple, but may require a good deal of practice. Revolve around, using one foot as a pivot. In other words "whirl," while looking at the sigil drawn on the palm of one hand.

to do its job. The sigil floats away from conscious awareness and into the depths of the subconscious. If you do not forget the desire, it is as though you have planted a seed, but keep returning to it every day to dig it up and see how it has grown. Naturally, an attitude that keeps asking, "Did it work?" serves to keep the desire and the sigil firmly fixed in the conscious mind and away from the subconscious powerhouse. Again, this is a "lust of result" problem. You need to forget what you want in order for the subconscious to get to work and materialize your desire.

Free Belief

Lust of result can be dealt with by taking on board another lesser desire and sigilizing it, after engrossing yourself in this lesser desire. The free energy of the lesser desire and its emotion is channeled into becoming more fuel for the original sigil and the purpose of the original sigil itself is forgotten. In this way, the free belief is directed toward the sigil, the purpose of which is not recalled by the conscious mind. Methods such as free belief often work well when there are a number of magical projects brewing, or when you are doing multiple workings for other people. This makes forgetting the purpose of the sigil easier.

It is always a good idea to keep a magical notebook in which you can record any important information about your magical work. There is no need for long-winded essays, brief notes will suffice. These notes can be extremely useful at some future date. This is one of the most important steps in building a powerful magical system that is truly your own. In Part II, you will learn how to charge your sigils with color associations, using eight types of magick that can be attributed to the seven classical planets, plus Uranus, which corresponds to the very concept of magick itself.[9]

---

[9] Ray Sherwin contends that, "The gnostic state has been entered when awareness of the body disappears and self is centered in or totally exterior to the body." Ray Sherwin, *The Book of Results* (Sheffield, England: Revelation 23 Press, 1992), p. 43.

6

THE MASTER RITUAL

THE FIRST PART OF THIS BOOK IS SPECIALLY DESIGNED to help remove confusion and misunderstanding, in addition to helping you discover your inherent power by using correct magical paradigms for sigilization and magick in general. The second part deals with the eight colors of magick and how you can easily apply these eight colors to sigilization rituals.[1]

The Essential Living Magick

In this chapter, we will look at the purpose and use of ritual. What is a ritual? What does it do? Which one is the best to use in any given situation? There are almost as many questions as there are rituals, for the subject is vast and complex. At the simple end of the scale you have spells and those absurd practices found in "instant" magick books, in which some supposedly 5000-year-old ritual is presented (in all

---

[1] I have used the same color sequence for the eight magicks used by Peter Carroll in his book *Liber Kaos* (York Beach, ME: Samuel Weiser, 1992).

seriousness) as being "effective" or of proven efficacy. At the other extreme, you find the curious practices given in the Key of Solomon (so-called) and the long-winded initiations of the Golden Dawn. Many aspirants to adepthood seek some "magick book" with all the answers. Only after fruitless searching do they learn that no such book exists. Transcriptions of ancient manuscripts like the *Enchiridion, The Grand Grimoire,* and *The Grimoire of Honorius* may look promising, but most are incomplete and so riddled with errors that they are little more than literary curiosities.

Nevertheless, these curious hybrids of Cabbalistic, Egyptian, and Christian mythology continue to intrigue scholars and inspire commercial plagiarists. Let me save you some bitter disappointment by explaining what a ritual is, why it can be effective as a magical tool, and how rituals work. The essential living magick is already part of your mind and simply needs to be awakened.

Magick is a pre-oral concept that manifests through symbols and imagery. The strength of magick is that it uses symbols or sigilized desires instead of equivocal human language. The desires epitomized in the sigil will elude the conscious mind but are accessible to the deep subconscious, where everything is possible. To make any ritual work, certain rules must be applied and respected. As you will see, magical rituals can be effective if common sense is allowed to prevail, instead of blind acceptance of the dubious writings and utterances of others. A magical ritual is simply a means of bringing together your mind, your emotions, and your imagination, so that they can be focused on a specific intention.

Ritual Intention

No ritual will ever be successful unless the intention is carefully thought out. Strange as this may seem, this simple fact is often missed, either through lack of knowledge or a presumption that the ritual itself actually does the work! All ritual intentions should be thought about carefully for as long as it takes to get this clear in your mind. There are many good reasons for this, the main one being that it helps to clear your mind of doubts and uncertainties that are bound to block access to subconscious levels. It also serves to help you know what you are doing and why you are doing it.

Suppose, for example, you intend to perform a ritual using yellow magick, which is fully explained in chapter 11. The first question to ask is why are you doing this? Look at your reasons carefully. Are you seeking to contact solar power:

- Because you are bored and it seems like a good idea?
- Because it is expected of you?
- Because you are simply curious as to what will happen?

Look at your reasons (intentions) to see if they are realistic and valid. Obviously, the ones given above are not, and the results will be proportional—because Input = Output. If only more magical practitioners would apply the ultimate question why to all that they do magically, the art would advance at an enormous rate and the efforts of the individual would be rewarded by time saved and the achievement of more decisive results. Think about your intentions. Contemplate slowly and deliberately, and consider all the possibilities. By doing this, you are giving information to your subconscious mind, for this incredibly powerful part of you is always alert and constantly storing up information in your memory. Even though you may not be able to fully recall this, it is always there for future reference—especially your final decision, which is then contracted into a sigil.

Words of Power

Before moving on to a complete ritual using one of the colors of the eight magicks, we ought to look at speech and those so-called "words of power." Anyone who presumes that the speaking of certain ancient words or divine names will, all by itself, cause power to flow or miracles to happen, is deluding themselves. This is nonsense! No word or statement contains power. The power lies within the mind of the person who speaks those words. As with equipment, words are tools used for the sole purpose of aiding concentration.

Let me give you an example. Say to yourself, either out loud or in your mind: "I feel good." Now say this several times with feeling. In other words, *mean* what you are saying.

"I FEEL GOOD."

Repeat this several times. Now, can you see the difference? You are using your emotions to put power into these words. Finally, repeat the words several times and use your imagination to see yourself pulsating with energy and goodness. Do this with conviction for a minute or so.

There is now a considerable difference between the original approach and the final one. The words have not changed, but the inner work has given power to these words. This is the real secret of words of power and the difference in magical work is astounding.

When speaking words you must put feeling and imagination to work or those words are dead and lifeless. This requires practice, but is well worth the effort. Always use your vernacular prime, which is simply your native tongue. Its potency in magick is unequalled.

Magical Incense

An authentic magical incense produces solid results only when its fragrance becomes, by means of association, the key to a particular level of consciousness. The emotional and environmental associations must be preserved by using each incense solely and strictly for its own ritual purpose. The use of a magical incense for everyday perfumery purposes renders it completely and permanently useless as a magical instrument.

All incense is nothing more than a plain smelly substance. The magick comes from yourself, deep within you. The incense itself is an aid, a focusing tool to narrow down and concentrate your will and mind so that you can will what you wish and where you wish. The best way to obtain the subtlety of fragrance from magical incense is to use loose incense. This needs to be burnt on specially produced charcoal blocks in some safe container. There are brass incense burners, or thuribles, available on the market. Chrome ice-cream sundae dishes make eminently suitable containers. You will also need charcoal blocks on which to burn the incense. Some brands of charcoal are "swift-lite," which means the surface is impregnated with saltpeter or potassium nitrate, allowing easy ignition. Other brands are plain charcoal. Pour a little alcohol or eau de cologne over them in a receptacle and then apply a match to the charcoal. Alternately, the block can be popped on the stove for a few minutes to ignite it. When lit and glowing, place it into the receptacle with fire tongs, not with your fingers! A little sand or fine gravel at the bottom of the receptacle will ensure easy cleaning. I, myself, do not use a thurible, which looks very nice hanging from its chains. I use stainless steel ice-cream dishes instead.

Gestures and Finger Positions

The principle of rituals is based on confirming an idea, a train of thought, by an external mode of expression. To put it another way, in a ritual you produce a train of thought by a gesture or symbolic action that will be designated as conjuration in magick. All magical processes and rituals are based on the primordial thesis of body postures, gestures, and manipulation of the fingers. Here are some simple examples: As you approach the door to the inner temple (see chapter 15) prior to opening the four gateways of powers, perform a gesture simply by putting your hands together and then drawing them apart as if opening a curtain. As you do so, imagine the door of the inner temple, the door between the two worlds, opening. When opening the four elemental gateways (see page 35) make to the east the gesture of the element of Air by raising your arms above your head, palms up, fingers out. To the south, make the gesture of the element of Fire by forming a triangle with your hands, as if holding a small pyramid to the brow. To the west, make a gesture of the element of Water, perhaps a downward triangle or pyramid held at the navel. To the north, make the gesture of the element of Earth, with your arms down by your sides, palms down, fingers pointing to either side. It is not possible to give exact directions. These will have to be created individually so that they express your thoughts, ideas, and intentions throughout the opening and closing procedure.

You should develop gestures and finger postures for erecting the Cosmic Sphere, summoning and sending forth power through the four gateways, closing the Cosmic Sphere, and any others you deem necessary. Learn how to devise suitable gestures and finger positions that embody your thoughts, ideas, and aspirations. As soon as the gestures and finger positions have become self-acting with your imagination, it will be sufficient only to perform the gesticulation and finger postures to achieve the effect or influence your subconscious mind. With regular practice, the whole thing will become automatic, releasing subconscious power in conjunction with your imagination, your body gestures, and your finger postures.

Magical Use of Sound

Sound is another useful, but little used, aid. Magical sounds fall into two categories: natural and musical. There is no need to stand in a stone circle surrounded by the sounds of nature, risking gales, rain, and snow. While outdoor workings do have their uses, alternative technology, like hi-fi equipment and a headset can be used. In fact, as with incense, music or drumming at the right tempo should be used. Both incense, sound effects, and sonics should be worked into the ritual at some convenient point, according to personal taste.

In order to aid concentration and help create the correct atmosphere or mood, bring into your temple physical objects that suggest the color of magick being worked. In the case of yellow magick, a yellow altar cloth, a yellow candle, and solar incense can be used to charge the sigil. Address each quarter and at each point, open the doorway using the appropriate conjuration. Yellow power will be allowed through into the ritual area and into the Cosmic Sphere. There are no hard-and-fast rules to follow. It is all a question of individual effort and ingenuity. Half-hearted attempts and blind acceptance of the written word are bound to produce poor results, so plan carefully and get involved, even if this does seem to take the edge off your enthusiasm for a while.

The Colors of Magick and Ritual Opening Directions

Each color of magick has a natural affinity with an element and therefore a natural magical direction within the Cosmic Sphere. In dealing with the colors of magick as they exist in their own right, you may wish to use the directions dictated by the color's natural affinity (see Table 1). For example, if you wish to do a working involving yellow magick, place the altar in the south and open the four gateways beginning with the magical direction of south. This will open the southern doorway and allow

Table 1. Colors and Directions.

Colors	Directions
Yellow	South
Silver	West
Orange	East
Green	North
Red	South
Blue	West
Black	North
White	East

yellow energy to enter into the ritual space, starting at magical south, and continuing in a clockwise direction back to south. At the end of the ritual, reverse the procedure. If you dislike this paradigm, simply open all your rituals beginning at east. At conclusion of the working, reverse the procedure.

The Rubric of the Master Ritual

Now is the time for magick, the time for mortal men and women to become gods and goddesses. Who among you dares to go on, who will turn back?

1. The temple is empty except for the altar at magical east. Its color depends on the color being conjured; it is all a matter of preference (see Table 1, page 63).

2. On the altar, place one candle in an appropriate color that illuminates the sigil (which can be seen from every part of the temple). Next to this, place an incense burner with the correct incense burning. Like all authentic incense, it should be burned on charcoal. To preserve its power and subliminal associations, it must be used exclusively for the purpose it is created. Pay special attention to lighting. Many candles or lamps may be needed, depending on the degree of brightness you require. Subdued lighting is best, and alternative technology, like a rotary dimmer switch, can be fitted to control the intensity of electric light.

3. Start the drumming tape. The equipment should not be visible.

4. Stand facing the altar and spend some time meditating on the sigil. After a while, perform the Sun/Moon-disc centering (see page 27).

5. Perform your opening formula. Erect the Cosmic Sphere (see page 32), and open the four gateways (see page 35) allowing the appropriate color into the temple through each of the the four gateways (see page 35).

6. Start to chant the mantra (if you intend to use a mantra). The drumming should begin about now. Incense,

drumming and/or music, and lighting should be arranged so that, once lit or turned on, they need no further attention for the remainder of the rite.

7. Start whirling and continue to chant the mantra. Visualize the sigil as firmly as possible.

8. Stop whirling.

9. Hold the sigil to the candle until it starts to flame. Place it in the incense burner and watch until the fire has consumed it.

10. Perform your closing formula. Use your imagination to see the gateways close, then close down the Cosmic Sphere (see page 33). Finally, extinguish the candles.

Now it is time to leave the temple, each with his or her experience, each with his or her own truth.

PART II

The Psybernomicon

THROUGH THE REMAINDER OF THIS BOOK we will examine the concept of color in magick. Associations are built up around colors, so we will examine different types of magick by their respective colors. Each color corresponds to areas of activity, normal and magical, that come under the heading of that magical color. The colors may be used in magical work as an aid to focusing your mind by varying the color as it is conjured through the four gateways of power to suit the intention of your sigilization ritual.

7

WHITE MAGICK

THE NATURE OF THE WHITE POWER IS SUDDEN CHANGE and magick itself. White magick also governs astrology, intuition, inventiveness, miracles, esoterics, sudden promotion, your wishes, willpower, convulsions, cramps, disagreements, spasmodic diseases, disruptions, fits, hiccups, and drugless healing.

White magick acts as a prism that helps you find your own personal magical color, sometimes known as Octarine.[1] Use white magick until you discover your own color for yourself. Uranus is the planet of the white power, the planet of origins and beginnings. How does anything begin? Quite simply, it begins in the mind as a thought. By thought, I mean an original thought—the type of thinking that is uniquely yours and no one else's. There is a world of difference between conscious thoughts—in other words, thinking "about" something—and pure original thought. Original thinking exists only for the

---

[1] Terry Pratchett, whose "Octarine" has become the eighth color of Chaos Magic. Terry Pratchett, *The Colour of Magic: Phantasy-Magic, Humor and Fiction* (London: Corgi, 1985).

person who conceived the thought and for no one else. This type of thinking is difficult to describe. It has to be observed and understood if you are to gain the full value of the white power. Every new invention, piece of music, and line of poetry is the direct result of original thought. There are those who imitate, and those who truly think. Everyone has this capacity, but few use it. This robs people of the opportunity to be themselves.

White magick is the power of being. "Being what?" you may well ask. Being yourself! To be yourself and realize your full potential, you must strive to be original—to be yourself. That's why the search for your "real" self is so important. At best, most humans are a poor reflection of everyone else's ideas. Confused and blind, they desperately try to make this image real, with predictable consequences. All failure and lack in life is largely due to people simply not being themselves. It is inescapable.

You may have heard the expression, "Why don't they think for themselves?" Think for yourself. Throw out dogma, superstition, and blind acceptance of the obvious and be yourself. It is the key to success. When you are being original—in other words, yourself—you draw on the vast potential of your subconscious mind. Stillness and being *you* produce power. Now you can see this explained in terms of magick. For magick explains everything to those who use it in original ways. I suggest that you forget all previously held paradigms and ideas about magick. You will find that, in reality, they were never any use to you.

Accept nothing without thought, both original and conscious. The general attributions of the white power are quite sensible—galaxies and nebulas are very apt. It was by looking up at our own galaxy, the Milky Way, that humankind really began to think about its place in the universe and its relationship with the stars. At first, there was no order or discernible pattern, but there was the beginning of many ideas and postulations. Original thinking was being applied. Something had caused these stars to appear and that something was deemed to be God. Later on, humans discovered that God also lay within their own being.

From a purely practical point of view, white power should be used in all self-searching operations. It is of the utmost value in finding out who you are and what your capacities are. Along with the visual image of galaxies or stars, you can use other attributions, such as a single point, representing the singularity found in the Big Bang theory.[2] In this model, all lines and geometric shapes emanate from a single point. As you move in any direction, you will draw a line, but the single point is the beginning. Uranus, or the white power, indicates how a person will deviate from the norm in a birth chart. Its aspects tell if a person will be constructive and inventive, or if they will be eccentric and disruptive. In any case, it shows how such a person will exert the ability to be different. White magick also indicates the powers of intuition and what is intuitive original thought. Intuitive thinking can be developed by the white power.

One further attribution is that of the magician, able to transform and/or transmute. The white power is your link to the Godhead, enabling you to become a dominant and authoritative, and occasionally even humorous, personality. In times past, magicians had to hide their faces. They became jongleurs, conjurers, or street magicians. They had to go underground during the persecutions and witch hunts for a time, with their real persona hidden and secretly kept. The surface transformation, however, was simply a means of portraying their secrets to those who recognized them.

All true magicians are capable of putting on a cloak of anonymity, of hiding behind some innocuous face when necessary. Magicians are contradictory figures. They are spiritual and adept, and show a balance between desire, passion, and real involvement in physical needs. They can be priests and, conversely, in need of a priest, although they do nothing that is actually sinful. The ability to change, as if by magick, to adapt to any person or situation, is a part of the magician's very special legend. They are also associated with Uranus and the white

---

[2] Gerald J. Schueler, *Enochian Physics: The Structure of the Magical Universe* (St. Paul, MN: Llewellyn, 1988), p. 196.

power. The white power gives you, your magician-self, the ability to be original and the ability to be self-motivated in the truest sense of the word. Magicians are set apart from the common herd by right. Little wonder that early magicians were credited with godlike powers. They are not gods, but have contact with the gods. They are not bound by religious affiliation, but are clearly aware of spirituality. It matters not what kind of spirituality they project, because they can be chameleons and respond to whatever is expedient.

Above all, the magician is a messenger from the gods to humankind. It is through the magician-self that those who created or formed this physical universe and our planet, and who experimented with human forms, can transmit their will and their guidance. The magician is an intermediary, a role that religions later adopted as their own, interceding with the sky people, as did so many of the great civilizations of the past.

In its more mundane aspect, white power indicates the psychic ability inherent in all of us. It thus represents psychic power and energy that can be recognized and used. This ability can be used in a small and personal way, or expanded to help others on a far larger scale. It is being used that is important.

White power will highlight this ability, whether this is recognized or not. Once the psychic link has been forged, white power will ensure that the flow of energy is constant and replenished after use. If the power is used for the benefit of others, this "topping-up" effect will continue. However, once any psychic power is used for other purposes, especially those designated as "evil," the power will still be given, but eventually will build up to a point where it will turn on the user.

The point is clear. When used for good and for the benefit of others, the magick we all possess within us will be controlled, as it were, by the white power. White power is the arbiter.

8

BLACK MAGICK

THE NATURE OF THE BLACK POWER IS STABILITY and limitation. It governs business matters, debts, land dealings, property, patience, self-control, endurance, depression, delays, restrictions, professional matters and one's profession, ambitions and career, the elderly, obstacles, falls, fears, inhibitions, chronic ailments, warts, and work.

The virtue of black power is silence. The black magicians are the quiet figures who do their work without fuss, using the robe of concealment. The key word of the black power is "understanding." Regrettably, black power is little understood, and is often classified as the great malefic. Without limitation, you would not have form. There would be impossible situations and you would have neither a body nor an environment in which to live.

Black power may often be viewed as restriction, but, as always, it is your choice. You can allow depression and negative thinking to bear down on you, or you can seek to understand why. Every effect has a cause and, within every apparent problem, is a solution. You can continue to beat your fists against obstacles, or you can learn to think them over. The lesson of the black power is that "all is as it should be." In other words, if you originate discordant and destructive ideas, these will eventually find form as restriction by your black Saturnian consciousness. You, as a human being, are responsible for who you are and all that manifests around you, without exception.

The black Saturnine power, or death-self, has two modes: the Grim Reaper with his scythe, and Father Time with his hourglass. When the sand runs out, the scythe begins mowing. The nature of the harvest depends on whether you have interacted negatively or positively with life. The truth of the matter is that you create your own troubles and experience the negative effects of your Saturnine consciousness. No one else is responsible. The reverse is also true. When you pursue true-self-seeking, wise ways, you will achieve perfect results. Cause and effect cease to be a curse and burdens become achievements, due to understanding.

Black power also links to the matured self, and leads to old age. The influence here is to stress the wisdom of age that time will bring. The taskmaster that the black power can be ensures that any acquisition of wisdom will be painfully earned. Black power combines these painful lessons with a benevolence that will make the hard experiences of life easier to live through. The philosophical realization of why it all had to happen will only come with advancing years. Then it will be possible to look back and see the complete picture of your life.

Contrary to popular belief, black Saturnine power is not the ruler of death. Death is not "the last enemy," but simply the cessation of the dance that creates the material illusion. Although death inspires the dauntless, it is also the element of change within the material world—in gardening terms, the maker of the compost on which new life grows. Only in its negative aspect is death the wrecker of monuments to human vanity and devourer of the materialists. We are all, human and beast, but spiritual stardust, and to dust we must return. Modern humanity is the only species whose brief and brutal existence is wasted in futile flight from this self-evident certainty.

The samurai warrior has no wish to die, but he does not fear death, therefore he prevails over the fiercest foe.

As material beings, we are the physical hostages of the Gnostic Demiurge, creator and ruler of the tangible world, known also as *Rex Mundi* and counted by all who pursue wealth and power. Those who declare "God is on our side" are often its most faithful, if deluded, acolytes. Cohorts of the Demiurge bear the insignia of religious, political, and bureaucratic office, and move in privileged circles, yet are enslaved by their own greed and gullibility. *Rex Mundi*, the King of the World, represents everything temporal and illusory.

Black power represents restriction, limitation, and consolidation. Black magick slows things down and encourages patience and steadiness. Black power is often associated with time. Always remember that uncontrolled expansion is not good. We need to apply the brakes to retain control and black magick is the power of control. Either you control its energy, or life is likely to restrict you.

9

BLUE MAGICK

THE NATURE OF THE BLUE POWER IS ABUNDANCE and opportunity. It also governs living joyfully, expansion, luck, optimism, legal matters, taxation, affluence, long-distance communication, journeys, and wealth.

Blue power is the source of abundance. It is also associated with Jupiter, the planet of joy, wealth, and opportunity for expansion. The position of this planet in a birth chart will indicate how a person is likely to receive or deny these benefits. As always, choice is the keyword. Everyone has this point of contact with abundance, yet few realize its potential due to wrong choice. If you are not experiencing lasting abundance, do not blame fate or classify yourself as unlucky. This is not true. Abundance exists for everyone. All you have to do is find the key to unlock the door—a door you have inadvertently placed between yourself and the eternal power of outpouring goodness.

Abundance comes according to the way in which you think. Think poverty and lack, and you effectively throw away the key. To contact and gain an abundance of everything that you need, all you have to do is to take the trouble to open the door and let it flow in. You can open this door by removing self-restricting thoughts. Blue power is expansion in every sense of the word, and expansion implies a free and unrestricted flow. Any thoughts of holding on to, or grasping at things, should be avoided, as such thinking implies insecurity. When you are truly attuned to blue power, you can never want for anything. You are secure, for abundant supply will always exceed the apparent lack.

Envy and greed, similarly, point to a complete lack of understanding of reality. Wanting to have what someone else has is the wrong approach. It distracts your thinking. Conversely, using this as a spur to better thinking is always fruitful. If you want to become rich, then do not begrudge the rich their wealth. Use it to inspire your wealth-self to be wealthy—not in exactly the same way, perhaps, but in your own way. Think rich, think wealth, think abundance. Remember, ask and it will be given. Nothing will ever be denied if you ask and believe in the laws of abundance. Depend on these laws and trust your inner powers of plenty. Then, allow this power to flow. Never allow the facts to dictate circumstances. The facts are largely wrong, for they are the product of the restrictive thinking of others. You will notice that abundance always manifests itself. For most of us, this means an "abundance" of lack or a condition of anti-wealth. The law always works: as you think, so shall you be.

To seek the true abundance of the blue power, think abundance and allow it to flow into your life. Remember that you are dealing with the principle of generosity and that this works both ways. A wise person can be truly generous, for they will never fear lack. There is no such thing.

Blue power is often considered lucky or fortunate. This is, perhaps, stretching the point somewhat. Blue magick represents expansion and opportunity. These may, at times, seem lucky, but only because new horizons have opened up and restrictions have been lifted, thereby bringing in optimism. Blue magick gives us scope for expansion and gain.

Use the appropriate correspondences, both physical and imaginary. See bright blue light flood through the four gateways entering your theater of operations. Those who seek personal advancement and financial benefits may find that the moral support of charging a wealth sigil is enough to invoke the "sweet smell of success." It is not a substitute for hard work and common sense, but a potent unconscious symbol of determination to acquire riches. Remember that a ritual performed by an experienced magician will work for the simple reason that the operator has the ability to contact the subconscious mind easily, and has practiced and devised a method of sleight-of-mind, using some form of gnosis, for example dervish-like whirling, and mastered the technique.

10

RED MAGICK

THE NATURE OF RED POWER IS ENERGY AND ACTION. It also governs ambitions, blood complaints, disputes, self-defense, dealing with enemies, personal energy, drive and stamina, getting rid of anger, aggression and other destructive impulses, and self-reliance. It can be a dark force, but not an evil one.

Red magick is the power of war, so they say. It is a safe bet that given energy, the human race will misuse it and then hold the results up as the accepted norm. War, killing, destruction, and other negative tendencies have no place in reality, let alone in magick, so let us forget about wars and strife and look at the real power of red magick.

Red magick represents a person's driving force. It is the energy that motivates a person into action—the warrior-self. Red power gets things done. It pushes aside obstacles using determination and strength. All acts of bravery and daring are governed by red magick.

Black power asks to be understood, and you must apply this understanding to the reality of life's energies and the red power, or you will face the consequences of cause and effect.

Wasted or uncontrolled energy is usually due to lack of understanding. It results in anger, unwanted force, antagonism, and even war. For every action, there is an equal and opposite reaction, according to the laws of physics. This is true on all levels. Life's energies should produce action along the right paths, provided that you think first and then act.

Red power, and its energy, needs and implies control, for every action must cause a result. Better to plan and organize than to be impulsive, for we are always responsible for our actions, whether mental or physical. Cause and effect are little understood, so we find useless excuses to cover up our lack of control, or we create convenient "escape clauses" so that we can blame something or somebody else—usually the gods, fate, destiny, or, if you really want to indulge in passing the buck, karma. The latter excuse is now an accepted belief pattern for millions of people who have not even thought about the concept, who have failed to realize the true implication of what they believe. To claim that it is not your fault, it is your karma, may seem like a good way to dodge the issue, but it is not. Neither is it any longer a valid excuse for not doing anything about life's problems. Any problems you have are truly yours. You caused them, in the same way that you are now learning how to cause far better things to happen. Thinking is the cause. Wrong thinking produces undesirable effects. Change your thinking and you are bound to change your life for the better.

Although the unconscious projection of malice and aggression is all too commonplace, genuine cases of real magical attack are rare. Most apparent magical attacks are not true magical attacks, but are quite often the result of acute paranoia induced by our own mundane afflictions or depression, negativity or frustration. Very often, however, it may prove expedient to devise some form of magical self-defense techniques. Even though it may never happen to you, it can do no harm to practice and elaborate on the Cosmic Sphere (see page 32), as it serves for magical protection as well as for centering. The stamp of individuality can only serve to help. Any magician worthy of the name will always be prepared for real or imagined imminent magical attack. It is interesting to note that even Jesus made use of cursing techniques as mentioned in the Bible, when he cursed a fig tree.[1] The key to the energies of red power is to stop, think, and then act in a responsible manner, using the assertive power of your warrior-self.

Red power may be invoked in many ways by using the magical paradigms given in previous chapters. These can, of course, be modified by using the correspondences for red magick and directing your attention to the upper point (crown). See the red power that is allowed into the ritual area. Feel yourself surrounded by this energy, then charge your sigil. All you need to do is to plan a series of rituals to last over a period of time—a week, ten days, or more.

---

[1] And Peter calling to remembrance saith unto him, "Master, behold, the fig tree which thou cursedst is withered away" (Mark 11:21). This, and all following Biblical quotes, are from the authorized King James Version of the Bible.

11

YELLOW MAGICK

THE NATURE OF YELLOW POWER IS BALANCE and vitality. It also governs the building of self-confidence, vitality and inner healing, healing others, discovering the real you, ego and self-image. Negativity, however, can also confer an overbearing, arrogant, egotistical attitude.

Yellow power is associated with the Sun. Its symbol is the six-pointed star that consists of two perfectly interlaced triangles. The symbol suggests balance and the harmony of opposites. These, in fact, are the keywords of yellow magick. It is also the realm of beauty and solar heroes. Like all other sacrificed gods of the yellow power—King Arthur, Odin, Christ, Osiris—they are destroyed, yet will come again. They are the once and future kings.

The Sun is at the center of the solar system, so yellow power fits in well with the ideas of our total self-expression using the subconscious mind. Just as the Sun is at the center of our solar system, so, symbolically, yellow power is the center, or nervous system, of magick. By using yellow power, we seek to be what we will. In other words, we strive to be ourselves, while drawing on the energies of all the other seven colors. This "being" is expressed as what we truly are, as opposed to what we think we are. Those who seek knowledge of the central ego and the ego-self should always look to the yellow power. It represents the center of our being, our inner selves, and our potential.

Balance and harmony are correct life expressions. Everything should be under control and in perspective. This is, however, a far cry from reality, in which most of life's tragedies and inner conflicts are due to our trying to be something we are not. Be yourself and all else will fall into place in perfect harmony. The concept of right thinking must be applied, for to indulge in negative and unbalanced thinking is to go against what you really are. Not only do you get the results of such thoughts, you also produce a clash of interests, with resulting inner tension. By seeking within, by using your subconscious power correctly, you restore balance and become your "self."

All natural healing of imbalanced conditions belongs to yellow magick, for what is disease and discomfort but a lack of balance. Yellow power helps put this right. It restores balance by adjusting energy patterns so that they once again conform to the way you should be. Disease, after all, is a condition of imbalance. Yellow magick is used to restore this balance, thereby healing the disease. Any situation that requires a restoration of harmony will respond to yellow power. Bear in mind that nothing is ever as clear-cut as this. There are always other factors to be taken into consideration. Generally, however, the theory works extremely well. Apart from healing, whatever is put into the subconscious mind will become a reality.

By seeking the truth about what you are and what you need, you will have all that is right and proper. A popular misconception is to view yourself as a "type." For instance: "I am a Sagittarius" or "I am nervous." If you tell yourself these things often enough, you will become them. Fortunately, choice can always be exercised and the process is reversible. Yellow power embraces all that you can become, so it is a mistake to narrow your field of possibilities and restrict your self in these ways. Be what you wish to be, using yellow power as your source of guidance.

12

GREEN MAGICK

THE NATURE OF GREEN POWER IS ATTRACTION and harmony. It also governs increasing money supply, personal magnetism, true love, personal relationships, marriage, pleasure, relaxation, social matters, and getting what you want in material terms. Both vices and virtues are present here, genuine unselfish love as well as lust and jealousy.

Green power is ruled by Venus and contains those energies attributed to her. In Cabbalistic lore, it is named "victory," a strange name to associate with green magick, the power of peace and love. At first glance, you may think that this should be attributed to red power. Let's look a little deeper. Green magick rules attraction and desire. Popular misconceptions suggest that you should gain victory over your desires. This is stupid. On the one hand, such a victory would be oppressive, which is hardly in keeping with green power. On the other hand, you can no more turn off desire than you can stop breathing permanently. It is the victory over misdirected desires that is important.

To desire is not wrong; it is what you desire that matters. There is victory in attracting into your life all those beautiful things you wish to have. There is victory in replacing lust with love, and there is victory in achieving or having the unattainable. To stoke up the fires of desire is to want with all your heart and, as you know, the heart, or yellow power, seeks to express all that is to be. The real victory is to desire all the things that you wish to have, purified of all harmful ideas. You can have whatever you desire, but take care not to do this in the wrong emotional or mental state.

To desire money is not wrong. To be greedy or desire someone else's money is. Green power is being misdirected and the laws of abundance have not been realized. Likewise, to desire another person without consideration of the other person's needs and feelings is also wrong. Life is ruled by give-and-take and sharing. You cannot force someone else to love you or to conform to your ideas. True love is binding, because the laws of attraction complement each other. Anything else is just a poor compromise. Rituals for love often fail for this reason. It is not love that is being sought; it is invariably control over someone else. It is far better to seek lasting love in new pastures, than to try to force another being to conform to an ideal.

The laws of green power teach us to give and take, rather like a flower. A flower needs to have its seeds fertilized, so it attracts insects by giving color, scent, and honey. So it is with humans. We attract in proportion to what we give out. If you express disharmony and greed, you attract these into your life. Purify your emotions and feelings and use desire power to bring into your life all those things you really need. This is the lesson of green power. Green magick is the symbolized power of the emotions.

Green power also governs your personal magnetism, or ability to attract. This attraction is not restricted to members of the opposite sex. Green power attracts all, for desire is the province of green magick, and desire is perhaps the most potent force humans have. Cultivate a desire for something and it is bound to be attracted to you. By desire, I do not mean hoping and wishing, or unproductive ideas. I mean desire. In matters of affection and love, desire is obvious and easily aroused. It is not as easy to apply this to an inanimate object, like a car. Yet, if you care to try this branch of magick, you may find it most effective.

Green power rules the emotions. The magical use of the emotions is called Orphic magick, which relates to the excitatory mode. As previously mentioned, music, scent, dancing, whirling, the arts, and self-love (laughing) are all ruled by green power. In truth, none of us are totally Hermetic or totally Orphic—we are a balance of the two. You will have to find out how much mental and emotional content to include in your rituals. Complex formulae, drumming, and accurate planning using the inhibitory mode may be right for one person, while music, scent, and whirling or dancing may appeal to another. Only you know the correct proportion.

It is important to remember that you can perform your rituals at any time. We are not ruled by the stars and the planets. These are just energies working to predictable tides linked with recognizable phenomena here on Earth. A useful paradigm is to organize a routine of lunar observations. Record your emotional impressions and, thereafter, perform magick during those phases in which you feel most powerful.

13

Orange Magick

The nature of orange power is communication and the mind. It also governs nervous problems (for example, stress, worry, anxiety, and so forth), improving the mind, speech and the ability to communicate, mind power, important agreements (loans and credit), lung complaints, dealing with neighbors and relatives, speech difficulties, concentration, decision making, local travel and charlatanism and trickery.

Orange power is Mercury, the messenger of the gods. Orange power rules communication. In other words, the way you speak and think. It is the power of the conscious mind. Correctly controlled emotions are essential if desire power is to work. Orange power helps you to use your mind as a tool for achievement. To sublimate the instinct is one of the keys to orange power. Right away, forget about intellectual brain-feeding or the accumulation of unnecessary facts and figures. Such ideas have no place in the reality of magick. You do not have to be clever or hold a degree in philosophy or astrophysics to be an effective magician or a balanced human being.

Unfortunately, society, which is often wrong, holds up intelligence as the criterion for growth. If true intelligence were implied, this would be alright. But this is not the case. When we pass an examination, we are deemed to be higher than others who have not. But what is an examination and what has happened when we pass? All we have done is memorize a variety of so-called facts and show that we have retained them.

The question is have we really learned anything of value and can we apply this knowledge? The blind acceptance of so-called facts is bad enough. For this to be the platform on which society is supported, and the way in which children are educated is unreal. Very few provisions are made for individuality of expression and learning needs. The mass-mind paradigm increasingly forces its unreality on people. Would-be magicians are perhaps more prone to conditioning than most. So often, they accept without question and subscribe to unfounded patterns of belief. This book acts as a magick mirror, wherein the pure see purity, the evil see evil, and the frivolous see whimsy, because it exposes both magical fraud and the false values of corrupt societies.

Naturally, there has to be some framework for learning, but this should be in keeping with the nature of orange power. There ought to be flexibility and encouragement to explore. The truth is simple, and so is the way to power. In the words of a great man: "When Jesus saw it, he was much displeased, and said unto them, 'Suffer the little children to come unto me, and forbid them not: for of such is the kingdom of God'" (Mark 10:14). He also told us: "Verily I say unto you, whosoever shall not receive the kingdom of God as a little child, he shall not enter therein" (Mark 10:15). The truth is simple to a child, before society forces us into a mold. For adults, the truth is often difficult to perceive, owing to the belief that life is complex.

The conscious mind is a tool. In the right hands, it is a tool for learning and applying that knowledge for advancement. It can be a source of trouble, nervous complaints, and utter confusion if it is rigidly educated to the wrong standard, because it is then at variance with the self. When used to plan, compare, examine, and make decisions around the needs of the self, it is functioning correctly, as a tool instead of an encumbrance. The ability to think and then direct the subconscious mind is magical. The need to indulge in book learning is largely self-defeating, unless a person has no other aims in life.

There is nothing wrong with knowledge if it can be applied or it satisfies a need. It is the ability to think in simple terms, however, that gets results, and that is what matters. It is essential to control the mind by seeking peace and then directing it into the appropriate channels. In other words, a mind full of confusion, darting about from one fact to another, will not produce concrete results or influence the subconscious mind beneficially. A quiet, orderly mind concentrating on an objective will enable you to plan out your campaign of action and help you sort out the wheat from the chaff, in magical terms. As you think, so you are. Quiet, calm, contemplative thinking gets results.

The mind is a magical tool. With magick, you are dealing with the science of using the mind. Magick involves a process of training and self-discipline, but the training must be done in stages, slowly and carefully, with a single-minded determination to succeed. You will be using parts of your mind that you did not know existed. Those parts are out of condition, stiff, and unyielding. They must be coaxed gently back to life, gradually brought to peak fitness. Many people leap into magical work with no thought at all of their mental fitness. They attempt to control the power of their minds before they have learned to control their mind themselves. They unleash a maelstrom of power over which they have absolutely no control. That power, once unleashed, knows no bounds.

Once you have learned to control the power patterns of your subconscious, many of the preliminaries of magick will become second nature. In temple work, neophytes must go meticulously through a set procedure of cleansing the temple, establishing contact with their inner selves, quarters or gateways, links with planets, god-form symbols, or whatever they may happen to be using. The adept can cover this entire procedure with very little preparation—perhaps just a single word or gesture. When you can do magick on a bus in rush-hour traffic then you will be making progress. (This is what my teacher told me.) A magician of many years training and control can dispense with the outward tools of magick, for they have learned to control the many levels of the mind.

Orange power is associated with speed and movement. It has a particular affinity with the mind, with quick thinking, alertness, wit, and the wit-self. Orange power is also a healer, but, in this case, through the use of surgery and medicine. In Mercurial terms, it is not by accident that the emblem of the medical profession is the caduceus of Hermes (the Greek equivalent of Mercury). Hermes, as mentioned previously, has also given his name to a particular branch of magick that deals with ceremonial and mental paradigms (the Hermetic arts) and relates to the inhibitory mode of gnosis. These largely appeal to those who use thinking as their prime motivation in magical work.

Although the orange power relates only in part to magical operations, full achievement is granted by the understanding and use of white power—the magician-self.

14

SILVER MAGICK

THE NATURE OF SILVER POWER IS RESPONSE and imagination. It also governs the solving of emotional problems and your responses to life's benefits, a better home, removing bad habits, control over your environment, domestic problems, gastric troubles, insomnia, passion, fertility, and sex.

Much as been said and written about the Moon and its magical lore, probably because the Moon rules our imagination. Silver power rules the treasure-house of images, the realm of illusion and dreams. I will not duplicate the efforts of others here, but rather will concentrate on the more useful magical possibilities of Moon imagery.

There are three ways in which the subconscious mind may be influenced: thinking (orange power), emotional desire (green power), and imagination (silver power, which corresponds to the Moon). The best plan of action is to use all three in proportion to your needs and abilities. Some prefer to use the mind. They are classified as Hermetic or inhibitory. Others prefer to stock up the emotions. They are classified as Orphic or excitatory. By themselves, however, neither of these will get results. You have to use some blend, and you have to use the imagination. You have to see in your mind's eye what you want or nothing can happen.

The language of the subconscious consists of pictures and symbols. Fortunately, this is partially taken care of in our makeup. Try thinking about something without looking directly at it and you will find a picture in your mind. The same applies to feelings. They both create pictures. The role of the imagination is to create the picture, rather than to draw on memory. To do this is quite easy. If you are good at visualizing, simply hold the picture or symbol (sigil) of that which is desired in your mind at the high-point or peak of gnosis during a ritual. Your subconscious will always respond and give power to this.

An apparent inability to create pictures in your mind is largely due to tension. The more you relax, the easier it gets. Forced visualization exercises are not recommended. To imagine something is natural and easy; you do it all the time. Cast your mind over any subject and you will see a picture, albeit briefly. The trick is to keep this subject in mind and allow the picture to form, while avoiding strain or seeing minute details. Relaxation is always the key to successful magick. Always remember that you do not have to keep your eyes closed to imagine. Do whatever comes naturally.

Silver power governs our response to life and our habits, so it naturally follows that progress is made when you discard those habits that are unproductive or bad. This area of life is well worth a study in its own right, and you will be surprised just how habit-bound you really are. One of the keys to getting results is that, when new thought becomes habit, it works automatically. The lesson is plain to see: change your thinking, encourage new, more desirable habits, and everything will change for the better and stay that way, automatically.

If things are not going well for you and there is discord in your life at the moment, it may be that you are out of tune with the cycles of nature and the elements. Especially a woman who is out of phase with the Moon can reachieve synchronization with it by sleeping in a place where it can shine on her. Synchronization must have first been observed between the lunar phases and the female menstrual cycle many thousands of years ago in societies living close to nature. If a female cycle is coincident with the phases of the Moon, she will be at her most fertile at the Full Moon. It is likely that sexually attracting pheromones may be exuded by her at that time, although these have not as yet been isolated.

Quite evidently, the Moon has a greater effect on the reactions of some individuals than on others. It also appears that the Moon exerts a more obvious influence on those people who are aware of it, its phases, and its position. It is evident that the Moon exerts an influence on the Earth and its people, but that influence is so varied as to defy generalization. It has also been demonstrated that the best way to get back into tune, or to become one with nature and the elements, is to regard the phases of the Moon. Become aware of them; go out and view the Moon at each of its four phases.

This procedure is best started on the night of the first New Moon in March. If this is impossible, start at the nearest convenient New Moon. Look up at the Moon for several minutes, perhaps using a small phrase such as: "I salute and conjure you, oh beautiful Moon." Wait for the New Moon. An aspectarian will show you exactly when this is.[1] Six Moons is a commonly accepted period for this type of work, which usually starts near Easter, so that your progress follows the growing period of spring and summer. Focusing on the Moon will help you to attune to the natural tides of energy. As you do, you will grow in strength and stature, because you will respond to life in much better ways. You will start to project yourself as you should be and others will start to respond favorably to this. You will develop better habits and lose those that have for so long caused you problems.

---

[1] You can use Llewellyn's *Moon Sign Book*. You can also buy *Celestial Influences* calendars, by Jim Maynard (Quicksilver Publications). In England, *Prediction Magazine* contains a lunar aspectarian.

As the Moon waxes and wanes, so you will rise and rest in perfect harmony with the tides of cosmic power. You will respond to the rhythms of life-energies and, so, achieve far more than was previously possible. You and the energies of life will come together in perfect harmony. Do not question; do not ask how or why; simply allow this to happen by opening your mind to this vast potential. Trust the power and it will be so. Relax when you perform this exercise. Let go and allow this power to work for you in the the unseen levels of your subconscious mind. Following this simple ritual for six months calls for self-discipline and organization if you are to avoid distractions.

Silver power can also be used to protect you against your enemies or those who wish to harm you. It can protect you from adversity of all kinds and from all quarters. Take your time in planning your rituals. The altar can be placed at magical west for the performance of silver magick. Don't forget to use silver-colored correspondences—altar cloths, candle holders, a silver candle. Use a good-quality lunar incense, using the same recipe every time. A useful variation here is to imagine that the crown has eight jewels set into it (one for each magical color). See the silver jewel begin to glow and get brighter. As you open each gateway, see this energy enter and fill the ritual space before the commencement of the ritual.

•   •   •

Now is the time to pause and consider carefully all that has been presented to you. Consider *everything* that has been written. Do not adopt one or two ideas that seem to appeal and then reject the rest. This is not the way to learn the truth or take control of your potential. In particular, avoid the temptation to rush ahead in the hope that you can extract the "nitty-gritty" and thereby find a shortcut to success. This is not possible, for the only real way to power is through the two-fold process of unlearning the erroneous and discovering the truth. This takes time and there is no easy way, despite the promises made in certain instant magic books.

Magical Techniques and Exercises

BEFORE EMBARKING ON THE FOLLOWING EXERCISES, you may find it extremely beneficial to make up a chain of about forty beads. These can usually be obtained from any craft shop. If you have a problem purchasing beads, use a knotted cord instead. The chain of beads can be used to show how many disturbances occur during your exercise period. It is a method commonly used by Tibetan monks. Every time you experience an intruding thought, move one bead. This will let you know how many interruptions there were.

Image Control and Nonthinking

"Nonthinking" is the ability to produce an absolute empty mind. Sit or lie in a comfortable position, on a bed or couch. Close your eyes and try to *stop* thinking. Let nothing happen in your mind. Hold this state of mind. In the beginning, you will be able to do this for only a few seconds. With regular practice, however, that period of time will increase. After the high-point of any ritual—the peak of gnosis—there needs to be a cessation of objective concentration. This is done with the understanding that, after having performed the ritual, the sigil must be transferred to the subconscious mind, as though the objective aspect of self acted merely as the designer or architect of a scheme and, when finished with the work, passed the plans and drawings over to the subconscious mind to fulfill.

After the peak of gnosis, dismiss the sigil from your mind. Transfer yourself into a state of nonthinking, preferably for about three minutes, but even one minute will do for the conscious mind to communicate your sigilized intention to the subconscious mind. If you have doubts or skeptical thoughts in your mind after your ritual, you will send to your subconscious mind the message that you doubt what you wish for will come true. This doubt interferes with the positive response. You must maintain an attitude of disinterested perseverance. Methods such as free belief often work well when there are a number of magical projects brewing or when you are doing multiple workings for other people. The purpose of this exercise is to enable you to remain in a nonthinking state for three minutes.

Image Control

The techniques of visualization or image control are not new. There has never been a time when they have not formed the very basis of magical training. Most of the so-called popular psychology books utilize the technique without going into details concerning the principles involved. Image control plays such an important part in magical operations that every opportunity should be taken to train this faculty. An earnest endeavor should be made to observe things and to be able to recall them in detail. Put some objects in front of you—a bottle, a cup, a pencil, a small ornament, or some abstract symbols painted on a card— a green square, a yellow circle, a red triangle, or a blue Crescent Moon.[1] Relax and fix your eyes on one object or symbol and try

---

[1] Alternatively, you can use the four tattva symbols and the methods outlined in Ophiel's book to develop this faculty in yourself. See Ophiel, *The Art and Practice of Getting Material Things Through Creative*

to remember everything about it—its color and shape. Then close your eyes and try to imagine the object. If it disappears, try to recall it.

In the beginning, you will only be able to do this for a few seconds. As time goes by, with regular practice, the length of time you can hold the image or symbol will actually build up until you can visualize whatever you like and hold it. Use the string of beads to help you keep track of the number of interruptions each time the object disappears. The purpose of the exercise is, again, to enable you to hold one object in your mind's eye without any interruption for between two and three minutes.

When you reach this point, you may practice holding the object or symbol with your eyes open. Check disturbances with your beads. When you can hold any object or symbol for two to three minutes without it fading and without interruption, you will have achieved the goal of the exercise.

Your Inner Temple

The following exercise is important from two points of view: it will help you relax and push away distracting thoughts, and it invokes a potent symbol that your subconscious mind fully understands. With patient practice, it is guaranteed to promote response from your subconscious mind in a way that is not possible by any other means. Symbols, as you now know, are the language of the subconscious mind.

Of all the magical operations, magical path-working is the most hypnotic in its induction technique. In path-working, the operator induces a trance in much the same way a hypnotist hypnotizes a patient.

As with all serious magical work, you must start by relaxing in surroundings that are conducive to magical work. This exercise may be done seated, or you may lie on the floor. Your eyes may be open or closed. Your goal is to build up in your

---

Visualization (York Beach, ME: Samuel Weiser, 1975), p. 86, which has been retitled: *The Art and Practice of Creative Visualization* (1997).

imagination an inner temple in which you can perform visualization with far greater effect. Contrary to popular opinion, the physical temple or magical workroom is, or should be, an extension of this imaginary condition. In short, a temple serves only to remind the magician of the real temple within the mind. The physical temple is also a workroom in which the magician may shut out the outside world and work undisturbed in congenial surroundings.

The purpose of this exercise is to learn more about it and yourself, to bring something up from your subconscious that will help. It is an exercise in attunement—something like visiting Alice's Wonderland. It will help you along the road to individuation. This is done by establishing attention points. These attention points are objects, situations, or archetypal entities. In this particular paradigm, they equate to the four doorways, to magical weaponry, and to a central pool. This pool becomes a valuable meditational aid. The vacuity of the pool helps you to concentrate, or rather meditate, and bring up information of a prophetic nature. If you wish to discover something, perhaps an answer to a problem, formulate this before you start your meditation ritual. When you reach the pool, think your question or problem into the pool. The pool can be used, like a crystal ball, to see into the future. It can tell you things and give answers to questions. You may substitute a crystal ball or dark mirror, but, by all means, don't forget that this is a substitute.

Meditation, unless a prelude to intelligent and determined material action, can lead to delusion. Practical magicians have always known this and acted accordingly. Meditation recharges your psychic reservoir. It provides a matrix of stillness in which forms from the realm of potentialities take shape. Until these forms have incubated and exploded into the world of material reality as physical facts, meditation is mere withdrawal. Meditate, by all means. Then *act!*

The Inner Temple Exercise

Find somewhere quiet where you will not be disturbed. Use subdued lighting and, if desired, burn a little incense.

Use soft music, if you wish. Sit comfortably and begin to relax. When you are calm and relaxed, perform the following exercise in your imagination. Light your central candle and erect the Cosmic Sphere (see page 32). Then see before you an Encircled Cross (see page 30). See this in front of you emblazoned on a door, and move toward the door in your imagination.

The door opens and you move inside. Once inside, look around to see what is in this place. You are in a large square room. You see the stone floor and the walls. In the center of this Inner Temple, set into the floor, is a small circular pool filled with water. In the middle of each wall is a doorway and suspended on each door, a magical weapon. In front of you (east) is a Sword pointing up; to your right (south) is a spear or Wand pointing up; behind you (west) is a Cup or chalice cast in precious metal; to your left (north) is a shield with a simple yet special design on it. Move to the eastern doorway. The door opens, revealing the element of Air—yellow energy. Move through this door and spend some time experiencing and attuning to this element. Allow ideas and images to come into your mind. Do this with all the other doorways in turn, seeing red at the south (Fire), blue at the west (Water), and finally, green through the doorway of Earth at the north.

Now go back to the pool in the center of the temple. Look into its depths. The pool will give you answers to your questions. Allow images to come into your mind. The duration of the pool meditation can be entirely up to you—five minutes usually suffices. At the end of the meditation period, simply close the elemental doorways in reverse order. It will be time to leave this Inner Temple. In front of you is another door. Go through it and you are back in your own time once more.

Before you forget any important points, write your impressions down in your notebook or magical diary. One day, they will become very useful. Always remember that you can enter this magical Inner Temple any time you wish. Eventually you will be able to make the journey in a few seconds. Perform this exercise regularly, until you are familiar with it. All it does is present to your subconscious mind a very specific symbol pattern. These particular symbols have a tremendous effect on subconscious levels, because they are universal symbols. They are very powerful. The more you work with them, the more you perform the exercise with an open mind, the more your subconscious mind will start to realize that you are giving it specific instructions and it will respond in its own way.

If you do see images, if you do notice anything during this exercise, make short notes and keep this for future reference. It is impossible at first, or almost impossible, to interpret these things on a conscious level. Moreover, it is certainly extremely difficult for anyone else to interpret them, because the symbols and ideas that come back tend to come back in a language best known to the subconscious rather than the conscious mind. They do not, therefore, make any immediate sense. If you make notes (you can keep them quite short—no need for long-winded essays), later, at the critique that always follows any magical operation, you can recount what you experienced. Some of these revelations are remarkable and will often confirm the contention that the collective subconscious is truly a transpersonal dimension. You will find that these notes can be extremely valuable. They are not, however, the object of the exercise. The object is to induce familiarity with the fourfold pattern of power. Gradually, with practice, this will build a bridge between your self and your subconscious mind, which, by the way, is the real "magician." By working the Inner Temple exercise, you will learn more about it and your self.

An Internal Meditational Charging Method

In contrast to the main theme in this book, I here present a paradigm that takes a very internal meditative inhibitory approach to sigil activation, using what is termed "measured gnostic conjuration." It is important to remember that all the same basic rules and procedures still apply. It is only the method of gnosis that has changed.

There is as much self-hypnosis involved in magick, especially the inhibitory gnosis directly induced by an operator. In fact, self-hypnosis may be considered the practical key to developing the inhibitory magical trance state. It therefore benefits any and all who practice magick to master self-hypnosis as soon as possible.[2]

Internal Inhibitory Paradigm for Sigil Activation

By now, you should be quite familiar with the Cosmic Sphere and the Four Gateways of Power. If not, you should become familiar with them *before* you proceed with this magical paradigm.

Using the concept of color magick and a sigilized intention, we will build up a hypothetical rite using yellow magick. Bear in mind that it is not the color itself that causes power to flow, but the associations made in your mind—in this case, the color yellow for charging a healing sigil. Prepare your temple space. You may wish to use two candles—one plain, to symbolize your subconscious power, and the other yellow, to symbolize the color of the magick you are using. You will need two vessels—one for burning your incense and the other for the symbolic destruction of the sigil.

Remember that you have to work within your imagination, in an imaginary Inner Temple, in this paradigm. Basically, this is a magical activity that is done within a nonlocal space accessed by your imagination. The idea is to create a consistent, realistic fantasy temple that includes all the symbolism you wish to encounter. You will enter this Inner Temple, opening the four gateways in such a way as to induce an inhibitory form of gnosis—one in which the operator is in a light state of trance known as "measured gnostic conjuration."

Perform the Sun/Moon centering (see page 27) and then erect the Cosmic Sphere. This serves to protect you and to contain the power that you are about to raise. Now imagine that you are entering into an Inner Temple (see page 102). Using your imagination, see a doorway before you and see yourself passing through that door, into the Inner Temple with its four doorways. (Those of you who have read my other books will

---

[2] Leslie M. LeCron, *Self-Hypnosis: The Technique and Its Use in Daily Living* (New York: Signet, 1970).

already understand this concept.) Add wording like: "I now enter the sacred dimensions of the Inner Sanctum." Then, direct your attention to the uppermost point. See the symbol of the crown and let your mind consider that which is God. Power flows from this point *as you will it*. See this as bright light in the appropriate color pouring downward in abundance.

Direct your attention toward magical east. See a door with the symbol of Air on it (the Sword). See and declare in some positive way that the doorway is now to be opened. See the door open and allow the yellow energy that came from above to enter your Inner Temple. See this happen and see the magical Sword inside the doorway. Enter the doorway in your imagination and absorb the magical weapon into yourself. This is done by feeling and imagining the Sword entering into your body, point up. Absorb the weapon.

Now return to the center of the Inner Temple using your imagination. This may be acted out with physical gestures. Do whatever you feel to be right. Direct your attention toward magical south and perform the same ritual procedure. See a door with the symbol of Fire on it (the Wand). Open it and allow yellow power to enter the Inner Temple, then enter in and absorb the weapon. Now direct your attention toward magical west. See a door with the symbol of Water on it (the Chalice). Open the door, see yellow power entering through the western door, and absorb the weapon. Finally, direct your attention toward magical north, seeing a door with the symbol of Earth on it (the Shield). Open it and allow bright yellow energy to enter through this door. Absorb the weapon. At this point, you will have acquired all four weapons, albeit mentally.

Now turn your attention to the symbol concept of the magical, or central, pool. Use your own ideas and preferences to make it the size and shape you want when you imagine it. You are going to *change* the image of the pool in a way that the subconscious mind will understand and act upon. Look at this pool and *know* you are about to use power. If necessary, declare this in some positive way, like: "I now call on my never-ending supply of subconscious power." Impress the sigil on the surface of the pool, then see the placid surface change into a huge fountain reaching high into the sky, gleaming with light and power. Hold the sigil firmly in your mind until you believe it has been emblazoned on your subconscious, or for a minute or two at the very least. Then see the fountain change to a calm pool again. Reverse the procedure by using your imagination to see and feel the weapons being returned to their correct doorways, beginning at north (Shield), then west (Chalice), south (Wand), and, finally, east (Sword). At conclusion, leave the Inner Temple, and destroy the sigil or prepare it for disposal. Then disperse the Cosmic Sphere and return to normality.

Building up the depth of trance can and does take some time. Returning to normal consciousness can be done more quickly. All this, of course, can be done as a seated meditation. It is far better, however, to combine physical action with inner imagination. With regular practice, you will find that you are capable of inducing a state of gnosis and maintaining it. This ability can only be acquired through training and practice. It will enable you to carry out these ritualistic manuevers in a magical operation, and still be able to hold your magical state of awareness. You should be able to quickly deepen the state, or bring yourself up to near-normal hypothetical consciousness when necessary, and to do all this while standing up as an active participant in the ritual. There is bound to be a teeter-totter effect in gnosis (trance depth) as you rise from passive to active participation. These techniques are not minor auto-hypnotic processes. They are a more direct vehicle, through which the magician can produce a desired effect in accordance with his or her will.

The following assumes that your intention has been decided on and rendered into a graphic sigil. Your temple, altar, and equipment have been prepared. Incense and a bit of drumming can also assist, but the ritual is best done somewhere where you are not likely to provoke an interruption. Unless you are an adept—in other words, you have complete confidence in your abilities—you are unlikely to succeed in performing just one ritual. Far better, in the early stages, to restimulate the sigil over a fixed period—say a week or ten days. You must decide on this for yourself.

The Ritual Rubric

Light central candle. Erect the Cosmic Sphere, then enter the Inner Temple. Face east, saying:

"To the east, the gateway of Air through which blow the winds of eternal change."

[Visualize the doorway.]

"I now declare this gateway open so that the yellow power may flow freely into this temple."

[Face south.]

"To the south the gateway of Fire and the triple flame of creative power."

[Visualize the doorway.]

"I now declare this gateway open so that the yellow power may flow freely into this temple."

[Face west.]

"To the west the gateway of Water and the land of images."

[Visualize the doorway.]

"I now declare this gateway open so that the yellow power may flow freely into this temple."

[Face north.]

"To the north the gateway of Earth and past mysteries."

[Visualize the doorway.]

"I now declare this gateway open so that the yellow power may flow freely in this temple."

The main body of the work is now carried out using the symbolism of the pool and fountain. This is also a good time to light the second candle, symbolizing the color of magick you are conjuring. It is also a good time for the drumming or music to start and to light the appropriate incense. Hold the sigil in your imagination and, if you like, chant a sigilized mantra. To end the ritual:

Close the Four Gateways of Power. Face north and say:

"Let there be peace to the north."

See door close and fade from view. Face west and say:

"Let there be peace to the west."

See door close and fade from view. Face south and say:

"Let there be peace to the south."

See door close and fade from view. Face east and say:

"Let there be peace to the east."

See door close and fade from view. Say:

"Let there be peace all around."

Extinguish color magick light and say:

"I now declare this temple closed."

Leave the Inner Temple and close down the Cosmic Sphere. Say:

"Let there be peace within."

Extinguish central light.

Conclusion

Magick starts in the mind by using symbolism, creative imagery, and gnosis. It uses some form of sleight-of-mind technique, as well as symbolic exercises such as the Cosmic Sphere and Four Gateways of Power. Magical equipment serves only to enhance this. Provided it is used in a commonsense fashion, it can most certainly help to promote the right frame of mind and thereby speed up results. The principles given in this book are sufficient to ensure success in practical terms, provided that they are read, absorbed, and applied. For my part, I can do no more than attempt to clear up misunderstandings, remove superstition, and give you ideas and models. The rest is up to you.

Magick is a vast and fascinating subject that may be studied in far greater depth along esoteric lines. The essential principles, however, remain the same. These principles are to be found within the pages of this book. If followed carefully and applied, they can lead you to a deeper comprehension of the true science of magick and an understanding of life itself. Never forget, however, that, before any real grasp of the universe is possible, you must first learn to master your own mind. Part of this task is to learn how to control the material side of life so that it becomes harmonious with your desires, rather than being out of control. "Evolvement" starts, not with self-flagellation, deprivation, or subservience to some god, but with self-assertion and the realization that life is for living rather than penance for supposed sins or karmic debt. In order to live fully, you must discover your *self*. This is not as difficult as some may have you believe, nor is it necessary for you to become part of a magical "elite" or be "initiated." The first real initiation is that of mastering the material by using universal energies and the vast potential of your own subconscious mind.

In the final analysis, you are what you *believe* yourself to be. This is unalterable, and up to now, has probably caused you considerable difficulties and hardships. The science of magick, as opposed to the perversions offered by the "magical boom" that is a symptom of the spiritual impoverishment of our age, can give you the knowledge to apply your beliefs using the vast power of the universe and the mediating influence of your subconscious mind. You must apply this; *you* must use this; *you* must discover the real truth about magick in your own way. For my part, I can only give the basic truth and useful models and ideas. You must do the rest. If this book has helped in some way, however small, I shall be truly happy in the knowledge that you have discovered reality and that the science of magick has advanced by proving itself.

BIBLIOGRAPHY

Carroll, Peter J. *Liber Null & Psychonaut*. York Beach, ME: Samuel Weiser, 1987.

———. *Liber Kaos*. York Beach, ME: Samuel Weiser, 1992.

Cooper, Phillip. *The Magickian: A Study in Effective Magick*. York Beach, ME: Samuel Weiser, 1993.

———. *Basic Magick: A Practical Guide*. York Beach, ME: Samuel Weiser, 1996.

———. *Candle Magic: A Coveted Collection of Spells, Rituals and Magical Paradigms*. York Beach, ME: Samuel Weiser, 2000.

———. *Secrets of Creative Visualization*. York Beach, ME: Samuel Weiser, 1999.

Cunningham, Scott. *The Magic of Incense, Oils and Brews*. St. Paul, MN: Llewellyn, 1987.

Faraday, Ann. *The Dream Game*. New York: Harper & Row (Perennial Library), 1976.

Fries, Jan. *Visual Magick: A Manual of Freestyle Shamanism*. Oxford, England: Mandrake, 1992.

Geddes, David and Ronald Grosset. *Astrology & Horoscopes*. New Lanark, Scotland: Geddes & Grosset 1997.

Gleick, James. *Chaos: The Amazing Science of the Unpredictable*. London: Minerva, 1997.

Grant, Kenneth. *Images and Oracles of Austin Osman Spare*. London: Frederick Muller, 1975.

Gray, William. G. *Inner Traditions of Magic*. York Beach, ME: Samuel Weiser, 1978.

———. *Magical Ritual Methods*. York Beach, ME: Samuel Weiser, 1980.

Harner, Michael. *The Way of the Shaman: A Guide to Power and Healing*. New York: Harper & Row, 1980.

Hine, Phil. *Condensed Chaos*. Tempe, AZ: New Falcon, 1995.

Hoffman, Kay. *The Trance Workbook: Understanding and Using the Power of Altered States*. New York: Sterling, 1998.

LeCron, Leslie M. *Self-Hypnotism: The Technique and Its Use in Daily Living*. New York: Signet, 1970.

Lee, Dave. *Magical Incenses*. Sheffield, England: Revelation 23 Press, 1992.

Ophiel. *The Art and Practice of Creative Visualization*. York Beach, ME: Samuel Weiser, 1997.

———. *The Art and Practice of Clairvoyance*. York Beach, ME: Samuel Weiser, 1969.

———. *The Art and Practice of Contacting the Demiurge*. Oakland, CA: Peach Publications, 1978 (self-published).

Orpheus, Rodney. *Abrahadabra: A Beginner's Guide to Thelemic Magick*. Stockholm, Sweden: Looking Glass Press, 1995.

Pratchett, Terry. *The Colour of Magic: Phantasy-magic, Humor and Fiction*. London: Corgi, 1985.

Schueler, Gerald J. *Enochian Physics: The Structure of the Magical Universe*. St. Paul, MN: Llewellyn, 1988.

Sherwin, Ray. *The Book of Results*. Sheffield, England: Revelation 23 Press, 1992.

Spare, Austin Osman. *From the Inferno to Zos: The Writings and Images of Austin Osman Spare,* vol 1. Seattle, WA: First Impressions, 1993.

U. D., Frater. *Practical Sigil Magic*. St. Paul, MN: Llewellyn, 1990.

Wilson, Steve. *Chaos Ritual*. London: Neptune Press, 1994.

Wylundt. *Wylundt's Book of Incense: A Magical Primer*. York Beach, ME: Samuel Weiser, 1989.

INDEX